# The Sun Shines
# on the Simmons Family
# in
# Savannah, GA.

(A Biography)

# The Sun Shines
# on the Simmons Family
# in
# Savannah, GA.

(A Biography)

by Louis Rivers, Ph.D.

Told to Him By
Walter Bruce Simmons & Others

authorHOUSE

*AuthorHouse™*
*1663 Liberty Drive*
*Bloomington, IN 47403*
*www.authorhouse.com*
*Phone: 1-800-839-8640*

*There are other Simmons Families in Savannah, Ga. but they are not related to the Simmons family of this biography.*

*Book front cover was designed by Auset Rivers, Grapic Artist*

*Published by AuthorHouse    05/19/2015*

*ISBN: 978-1-4918-2278-4 (sc)*
*ISBN: 978-1-4918-2277-7 (e)*

*Library of Congress Control Number: 2013918051*

*Print information available on the last page.*

*Any people depicted in stock imagery provided by Thinkstock are models, and such images are being used for illustrative purposes only.*
*Certain stock imagery © Thinkstock.*

*This book is printed on acid-free paper.*

# Table of Contents

## Part One

Meet the Simmons of Savannah, Ga.

## Part Two

The Sun Beams On The Simmons Family

# Part Three

Special Celebrations in Recognizing the Simmons:

# Dedication

This biography is dedicated to reliving the many **inspirational and precious moments** we lived with the Simmons Family in the Old Fort **and elsewhere in** Savannah, Ga. from 1920 to 2012.

# Acknowledgements

Writing this biography has taken more than five years to complete. In that time, we have celebrated Simmons' homegoings. Nonetheless, we must and want to acknowledge that this book could not have been written without any of them.

Ephriam, Nellie, and Jeannie contributed information up to their sunsets.

We thank **Eunice Wright, Clifford Harwick, and Dr. Lester Johnson** for their letters sharing their sentiments of the Simmons.

My daughter, Luisa Filippi, my extended hands, legs, and vision stayed indispensible. Loria Stanley, my youngest daughter, and typist patiently typed and retyped pages of several drafts until I got it right. We are also grateful to Thomas Southwood and DeShawn Hatcher for their expert help with our photographs and other graphics.

Above all, however, we thank Walter Bruce Simmons (fondly called "49") for his tremendous patience and unusual ability to discover "gems." When others were ready and willing to defer completing this book, he wouldn't give up. He kept his spirit and trust in high degrees. Without him, this book would not be in existence.

We also congratulate others for whatever contributions they made to this **indispensible biography**.

We are also grateful to Graphic Artist Auset Rivers, my granddaughter, and others for the book's front cover design.

# A Foreword

By

Diane I. Wilson

Chairperson of The Black Studies Department

Of

New York City College of Technology/C.U.N.Y

Greetings, all you avid readers, it is my honor and privilege to introduce you to the mind and memories of Dr. Louis Rivers. I am a long time friend and former colleague of Dr. Rivers. I have always known him as Lou the teacher, the writer, the critic, the curmudgeon and friend. I helped to organize his retirement party celebrating his 50 years of teaching, half being spent teaching speech at New York City college of Technology of the City University of New York. It has been since his retirement that he has had the time to flourish as a writer and author. Every Christmas Eve, at a party given by a mutual friend, I could expect to get some interesting and relevant reading material. The first I received with his authorship was a collection of original One Act plays titled, **Opening Doors.** I have always been inspired by Lou for his love of the Old South as he knew it; a Black South built from the ashes of the Civil War, fortified in the depths of the great Depression and brought almost to fulfillment during the Civil Rights Era. Lou speaks of his hometown of Savannah, Georgia like it is an old cherished photograph. The very thought brings forth waves from childhood to adult memories of people and places. In this biography of memories, the main characters are the Simmons family.

It was Lou whose stories of the south spurred me to spend a week in Savannah five years ago. It was all that he said it was and more. When entering Savannah one instinctually would leave their stress at the City Line. Old Spanish Moss laden oak trees, black wrought iron works and the slow moving elegance of Savannah took my mind far from the glass, steel and concrete of New York. In this biography Lou reveals in the Simmons' South, the family values of African America. This was the South of my grandparents, passed on to my parents and finally to me.

If we could go back in time, would we find our past as we remembered it? It is fixed in time never to be altered by the present or the future. Memories of bygone years should be those worth remembering, preserved to sustain us in the here and now.

What makes this biography exciting is that it reminds me of the stories my mother mold me about life growing up in the north (or "up south") during the same time frame. My mother said that they never knew that they were poor because everyone around there was in the same boat. How about Soul Food? That's a term used only in recent years. We just knew it a Home Cooking, yum. It this book, Lou is trying to explain to his readers and to himself what, or better still, who made him the man he sees himself to be. He uses terms we are accustomed to using today. Nowhere appears the words negro or colored. Lou uses the members of the Simmons family to explain generational progress in spite of historical discrimination. What I find that readers will find most striking about this book is that it is more than a biography of one man and one woman's devotion to raising a family against all odds. It is a biography of a family much in the style of "Roots", a success story of one particular southern Black family. The story of the Simmons family conveys the need for all African Americans to embrace their southern roots with pride and remembrance. This biography of the Simmons family encourages families everywhere to hold on to their memoires, their stories, their photographs as a way of honoring our fore parents and mentors who instilled in us the need and the desire to preserve the time we have left here on earth, so that they should not be forgotten. How many of us can actually trace our genealogy back three or more generations? Unless someone like Dr. Rivers whose memories intertwined with those of the Simmons', a families past would have been lost to us forever. If every life is supposed to be precious, then every life is worth remembering.

The world of Wally Simmons and his family was the world best remembered by our mothers and fathers who grew up in the heart of Dixie. Lou offers the reader a detailed explanation of what sustains a person, a family, and a people. How, if build on a firm foundation, one cannot help but prosper.

I am a lecturer of African art, cultures and traditions. Many of the old traditions come to light in the biography, many of them which stem from many years of lecturing on traditional African style funerals.

What I find remarkable is that each generation of the Simmons family not only contributes to the betterment of their family, neighbors and community, but comes to represent true pillars of the community and what makes the family unit work. Each man and woman in the Simmons story maintains his or her family values and passes them on to the children.

I found Dr. Rivers' method of having family members for them is an interesting format not usually seen in biographies.

I encourage you all to read about the lives of the Simmons family. It may help give you ideas on how to record your own family's history. If not, then like in the case of Dr. Rivers, find a family that you do like and set about searching out those memories that blend with yours. Start your search engines now.

Diane I. Wilson

# Part One

## Meet the Simmons of Savannah, Ga.

# 1

# SunRises And SunSets In Savannah, Ga.

In Savannah, the most beautiful moments of day exist. Savannah days have always inspired me to realize living in Savannah was poetic, seeing life emerge, developing, and diminishing into another dawn, a new beginning day, again twilight—spreading across Savannah, **enveloping all things**—completely—deeply—affecting the significance of largeness and smallness, hardness, goodness, even greatness!

I am the author, a Black African American who grew up in Savannah, Ga.'s Old Fort, an eastside ghetto, for Geechees. Geechees, former slaves (their off-springs too) hailed from the Sea Islands in South Carolina. We Geechees speak Gullah, a mixture of English and African dialects.

As a boy, I grew up <u>happy</u> and <u>proud</u> being Black, living with other Blacks in the Old Fort. Some may have felt inferior (no one ever expressed it to me) ever that being Black was ugly.

Black Savannahians concentrated on surviving—learning how to get food; how to keep safe, maintain health; know how to make love; how to sing, dance and be obedient to God and "the law"; and to play great sports. We, Black Savannahians, laughed a lot as we enjoyed the Sun rays and the colorful Sun settings at twilight. We Africans loved the Sun.

In the Old Fort, we made the Fort our African Village. Despite an overall rejection and restriction by Jim Crow oppression, we strengthened our defiance of Jim Crowism by building our appreciation of our own creations or holiday celebrations, our "soul foods" dishes composed of what oppressors did not select to eat. We created our own music and dances, and we made our own conventions that allowed us to stay alive. We struggled as we realized our own social and personal visions.

We gave respect to members of the Old Fort Village. Names of certain families, automatically engengered respect. We labeled them "good families" "decent families", "respectable families", and the family of Walter Wallie Simmons was always in the top of the Old Fort's list. We accepted the Old Fort's social ingredients as we learned deeply to accept the richness of Black life. The Old Fort was our African Village, and we felt blessed to be its children.

1930 was the morning year of my generation (Presently I'm 89 years old). 1930 also introduced the village to the Great Depression, the madness of dictators—Franco, Mussolini, and Hilter. It also began the presidency of America's greatest president since Abraham Lincoln, Franklin Delano Roosevelt.

# 2

# Wallie Simmons Was an African Prince!

It was in 1930 when I first perceived Mr. Walter Wallie Simmons to be a **real African prince.** Since then I have often recalled my personal and favorite picture of Mr. Simmons—a tall, athletic, Black, handsome man. While he was standing tall, he bent from his waist to tie his shoelace. He placed his foot on the edge of a straightback chair to tie the lace of his left-foot shoe, a tan shoe, almost the color of a tangerine, the same similar color and style of a shoe my father wore; and shoes my father's friends wore; all from St. Helena, S.C. Those shoes, ankle-top shoes built thicker and stronger at the toes told me Mr. Simmons was like my father, and my father's friends—"real country"—and like my father and my father's friends, Geechees—all—from St. Helena or another of the South Carolina Sea Islands.

I remember being with Mr. Simmons in his living room, on East Oglethorpe Avenue. Why was I there, I do not recall, but I remember. I was there with him and another male adult. When Mr. Simmons had tied his shoelace, he rubbed my head affectionately, and we three men left the room to go to the frontporch. Mr. Simmons and the other man said all they had to say. Then they said goodbye. Mr. Simmons walked full of purpose and pride towards Price Street, and the other man, who held my hand, walked with me in the opposite direction towards East Broad Street. It was a summer day, and the heat was schotching.

To write this biography of the Simmons family is indeed an honor for me. The Simmons family of the Old Fort is supreme, one of Savannah's long lived African American working class families. They exemplify the best, the most ideal models of an African American working class family anywhere in America. They have struggled, across the years—through World War I years, then the Great Depression, and World War II Years, the Cold War Years, and through the Civil Rights Struggles Years—through all the **bitter years** of Jim Crowism, through its many forms and levels of racism, discrimination and segregation—and yet **the Simmons have survived,** not ever forgetting their obligations to foster and to support the ongoing struggles of African Americans everywhere **to be free** to construct their own Self Determination.

This Simmons biography is a recorded affirmation of African Americans who are a mighty nation of people, second nor inferior to any other. I know the Simmons. I've known them from childhood to the present.

I went to East Broad Street Elementary Public School with the Simmons, then to Beach Cuyler Public High Schools with the Simmons, and I attended Georgia State College (Now Savannah State University) with the Simmons, and together we attended the same church— St. James A.M.E. church, and I saw the Simmons boys, John, Frank, and Walter B. play outstanding sports in Savannah's Crawford Square—football, baseball, and basketball. I'm told Jeannie and Juanita also played outstanding sports.

# 3

# Meet Mamma Dolly Grayson

My incomparable "Play Grandmother" as she taught me to think of her cast me as her standby, her play grandson. "Old Head" she called me. I was for her a third son. Willie and Johnny, her own two sons by birth, now men, had already moved to live in Harlem, New York, and both my blood grandmothers were already dead. It didn't matter. No one alive (or dead) could compare favorably to Mamma Dolly. She was my beautiful grandmother, whose smooth skin displayed her vanilla wafer color. Both, physically and spiritually beautiful, she loved me as deeply as I loved her. And because she came from Bluffton, that city unseen, became for me a part of heaven. Even though I realized Bluffton was the place where there was no high school built for African American youth.

Time after time, Mamma Dolly described to me different animals on her father's Bluffton farm, telling me in details how a goat or pig died differently from a sacred sheep or lamb. For her a lamb held sacred secrets. She imitated the dying sounds animals made, all except the sheep or lamb which died quietly, turning its head from side to side until dead.

Mamma Dolly described and compared Bluffton's sunrises and sunsets to Savannah's and she likened Savanah's cool summer days with the air of Bluffton's rivers and marshes. She also spoke of Bluffton's people being kinder and brainier, and more handsome than other Geechees from St. Helena or Hilton Head. I believed her deeply.

My readings of Bluffton also told me Bluffton was located on a scenic bluff that overlooked the May River in South Carolina which is low country. There with Hilton Head and Ilses of Palmes, Bluffton is miles of sandy coastlines, beautiful sea marshes, quiet lagoons, with a climate average temperature of 80 degrees in the summer and 60 degrees in winter. Its streets are shaded by stately oak trees draped in delicate curtains of Spanish moss. Bluffton exudes Southern quiet dignity. Its communities are planned and designed with its churches, houses, little shops, restaurants, schools and neatly sculptured golf coasts.

Walter Wallie Simmons became an African prince when I transported his image to real and imagined scenes. I saw him in time and places where he never was. For example,

I placed him in a special picture that hung from Mamma Dolly's dining room wall. The picture was an African American man dressed in a U.S.A. Army World War I uniform. He stood at attention as the American flag waved in the space behind him. Who or what man posed as the soldier I do not know, but from the first time I saw that picture, the soldier became Mr. Walter Wallie Simmons, brave, handsome and Black. I think now that picture was made to promote and reinforce pride and patriotism in World War I efforts.

**One of my comforting memories is that of Nellie Simmons, Walter's third pretty daughter who was my favorite Sunday school teacher at St. James A.M.E. church, especially, when she sat at the piano to teach us children new songs to sing at the church's Children's Easter Sunday Programs.**

We learned to sing:


"He arose

He arose

He arose

From the Dead"

    And

"Jesus loves me

This I know

For the Bible tells me so"

# 4

# The Simmons Began In Okatie And Bluffton, S.C.:

My research findings for this Simmons' biography begins in 1908 on a March day!

Then Walter Wallie Simmons of Okatie, S.C. married Daisy Alice Simmons of Bluffton, S.C., the sixth and youngest daughter of Frank and Jane Ford Simmons of Buffton, S.C.

They resided in Bluffton giving life to their first four children—Marie, John, Nellie and Bessie. (The Simmons, however, printed the Simmons Family Tree beginning with Daisy Alice's family beginning with the marriage of Frank Simmons, a farmer, married to Jane Ford, a midwife, born in Charleston, S.C. Frank Simmons met Jane Ford in Bluffton when she'd migrated to Bluffton. Frank and Jane married began the present Simmons' Family Tree.

(See, <u>The Simmons Family Reunion</u> in appendix A)

# 5

# Bluffton, South Carolina Was a Special Place!

From what I have read and heard about Bluffton, South Carolina, Bluffton was and is a special place where Mamma Dolly grew up pretty and protected. It is a masterpiece of positive living designed by both nature and men. Never having been in Bluffton, S.C., in person, I went there in mind, imagination, and feelings, many times, and I always found Bluffton a place of poetry. As I've said before, Mamma Dolly said "Bluffton is a piece of heaven drifted down to rest quietly on a bluff".

Growing up in Savannah, Ga., I received romantic impressions of Bluffton from Mamma Dolly, whom I thought was the most precious human being alive. It was Mamma Dolly Grayson, who painted me pictures of Bluffton as a piece of heaven left on earth by angels.

Walter Wallie Simmons, African prince, physically and emotionally, reflected Bluffton, South Carolina, and so did Daisy, the mother of Walter's children. Mamma Dolly knew the Simmons, respected them, and worshipped with them as members of the A.M.E. faith at St. James A.M.E. church in Savannah, Ga. Walter, Daisy, and Mamma Dolly first joined Campbell A.M.E. church in Bluffton (See appendix B)

I also remember Easter Evening Programs at St. James A.M.E. church where I received applauses and extra boiled colored eggs for reciting with loudness and clarity long poems. At the end of my recitation, I always looked for Mamma Dolly, Miss Sadie Moore (cousin to the Simmons) and Mrs. Daisy Simmons who usually sat together in the same pew or pews nearby. I was softly hugged by these ladies and other women who sat nearby.

# 6

# The Simmons Became Followers of Richard Allen before Coming to Savannah!

When Walter Wallie Simmons and Daisy Alice Simmons moved to Savannah, Ga. in 1920, with their first four children—Marie, John, Nellie and Bessie, the Simmons came already confirmed A.M.E. Christians. They both had already joined Campbell's A.M.E. church in Bluffton, S.C. They had become committed to Jesus' teaching and to accepting the blessings of pride and courage of being African (See Appendix C) Mamma Dolly too was a steadfast A.M.E. Christian. Without ever saying it, Mamma Dolly implied she felt her husband's birthplace, Hilton Head, S.C., and his Baptist church faith stood inferior to her African Episcopal discipline and tradition. Like all other African Episcopal Methodists, Walter Wallie and Daisy learned early in their conditioning and education, the A.M.E. church was founded by Reverend Bishop Richard Allen, a Delaware slave, who had purchased both his and his wife's freedom.

Richard Allen, chief African role model, founder of the Free African Society, lived his vision to lead African Americans to develop as whole men and whole women and to cultivate top-rate leaderships among African Americans.

In 1794, Richard Allen led in founding Mother Bethel African Episcopal church in Philadelphia, Pennsylvania rather than worship in a segregated church. (Richard Allen's body is enshrined in the basement of the church)

In 1816, Richard Allen became the first bishop of the A.M.E. churches, and he preached against sending free Blacks to colonize settlements in Africa. He said African Americans had been stolen from their mother country and brought to America. "We have and made fortunes for thousands . . . This land which we have watered with our tears and blood is now our mother country" . . . (Marcella Thum, USA Guide to Black America, pp.59-60)

Like all other good African Americans, the Simmons marched in a prominent parade of determined Africans with such African Americans as Frederick Douglass, Lucrateu Mott, William Stall and James Forten.

It was Forten who served in the Revolutionary War, and who joined Richard Allen in raising a force of 2,500 free Blacks to defend Philadelphia during the War of 1812. (Marcella Thum, U.S.A. Guide to Black America, pp. 296-297)

It was also Forten who spoke out at Mother Bethel A.M.E. church in Philadelphia against the idea of resettling slaves in Africa. He also helped to raise the funds for William Lloyd Garrison to found the Liberator, an Abobnist's newspaper.

# 7

# June 9, 2007—Remembering the Simmons!

**-A-**

"I, Clifford Hardwich, of Savannah, Ga., remember the Simmons family of Savannah, Ga." I was born and reared in Savannah, and I always knew and respected the Simmons family, all my life. They were and are a great African American family and their mother, a matriarch, the late Mrs. Daisy Alice Simmons, was **a great lady** and **an ideal Mother**, and we, other folks' children, as all her own, loved her dearly.

"The Simmons were religious but not religionistic. They are producers of outstanding educators, athletes, and professional civic workers."

**-B-**

**Remembering the Simmons by Eunice Wright of Ricon, Ga.!**

"I will always remember the Simmons of Savannah Ga. They were and are a fine family who believed in education and in playing competitive sports. I feel we were blessed to have known the Simmons and to have associated with them. I first met the Simmons when I first met Juanita Simmons, the youngest of the girls—Marie, Nellie, Bessie, Alma, Eugenia, and Juanita. There were four boys-John, Ephriam, Frank and Walter whose number was "49" printed on his football jersey. We all called him "49". It was in 1946 when I first met Juanita. I met her at Beach Cuyler High School in Savannah, Ga. We were both in 10th grade (after I had graduated from Haven Home School in New Haven, Ga.)

"Juanita and I were enrolled in the same homeroom class with Dr. Philip Cooper as our homeroom teacher."

Juanita, whom we tagged "City Girl" and I became fast friends. We also became members in Demoisella's, a high school social club with an emphasis on fashion. Miss Dorothy Ury was our club's advisor. Juanita, being the youngest of the Simmons, enjoyed the others' indulging generosities which cast her as "a fashion example."

Being a Simmons, Juanita followed her brothers in liking and playing competitive sports. John, Frank and Walter, all outstanding Athletes, enjoyed playing competitive sports, and they were all hailed for excelling in sports.

Juanita was no different. She joined Beach—Cuyler High School basketball team, and she persuaded me to join the team too. Not being a player committed to sports as Juanita, I left the team after a few weeks when I had joined the team.

"I remember our friend Christine Jones had also joined the basketball team. She was like Juanita, a good player."

I remember I was honored to meet other Simmons of the Simmons family. They then lived in a big house on East Broad Street. On Juanita's invitation, I spent several days as her house guest.

"Come to think of it now, Ella Jones, another friend, also played basketball. Lola Dixon, Carloyn Grene Lewis, and Gloria Oliver, all played basketball. They were also members of Demoselle sisters and wore royal blue skirts and white sweaters."

"Boys we thought cool were both scholastic and Athletic. They were Frank Baldwin, Edward Ellise, John Gantey, John Morris, Albert Pinckney, Walter Simmons, Juanita's youngest brother, Baston Williams, and Edselle Robinson. These boys didn't wear saggy pants with big shirts."

"It saddens me to realize Juanita is no longer with us. Others are also gone, but I was and I am still grateful for the time I shared love and respect with Juanita Simmons and the Simmons family."

"I should tell you I graduated from Savannah State University in 1960 and I remained on the staff as secretary until I was commissioned to serve in the U.S. Army until 1979 when I retired".

# 8

# Remembering Papa!

"On the day Papa became most ill, he'd walked from River Street and Bull Street to the park on Abecorn Street near Broughton Street. Exhausted, Papa sat down on a park bench. He could go no further on his own. As I've said, in those days, Blacks could walk through parks, but Blacks sitting in parks was discouraged."

"Someone who recognized Papa telephoned the grocery store next door to our house to tell us of Papa's situation. There was no automobile available and no taxis for Blacks, so my brother, John, and cousin, Ephriam, rode a bike to take Papa home. Somehow they balanced him onto the bike to ride him home. He never recovered. Papa died when Juanita and I were first graders at East Broad Street School. Miss Gertie Davis was our teacher."

"When school time had come again in September, I had become ill and couldn't attend school; so I was late beginning school. Mamma learned Ms. Davis would not teach first grade until January. So not until January Mamma took me to school—at the mid term. Remember we used to have mid-year promotion. Ms. Gertude Davis was Mamma's preferred first grade teacher and she wanted me in Ms. Davis' first grade class. While we waited for the mid-term semester, Mamma enrolled me in a preschool class. So I actually got promoted to the first grade in the same year Juanita started school in first grade. She and I then remained classmates until we graduated from Beach Cuyler High."

"I recall Papa's funeral at St. James A.M.E. Church. We then motored over to Okatie for the burial in Millen Hole Cemetery where Papa's father and one sibling were already buried there. The cemetery purchased then by a person who had the cemetery fenced in and forbidden to more burials. The cemetery became a cow pasture and became infested with red bugs. This discouraged visitations to grave sites, and eventually, the grave yard with Papa's grave site has remained lost."

"Nonetheless, we do remember Papa with prayers of thanksgiving and gratitude. We remember how much his family meant to him and how he managed to provide adequately for us during the stressful days of the Great Depression."

"We remember Papa as always being even tempered and blessed with loving patience and understanding when he dealt with us and our problems. While he might have been a softe with his children, Papa was a very strong male figure, one that we loved and respected."

"As we think back, one of our most vivid memories of him is this experience: You may recall the days before central air and heating. There was one room in the house with a heater or fireplace where the family gathered on cold mornings. Papa would start the fire on cold days before he'd call to us to come downstairs to warmth while we dressed. Papa would always sit or stand as far away as he could from the heater as we rushed in with our clothes to warm and to dress. Funny thing—we couldn't see the heater because we were right on top of it and had it surrounded. As the heater grew warmer, then hot, we moved back. Soon we were all the way back. Papa would laugh."

"There is no surviving picture of Papa. We may have found one of his father; however, we do have pictures of Papa's mother and several of his siblings."

"We always knew when Papa had cautioned Mamma to lighten up on any punishment she had declared worthy for some infraction one of us had committed. Mamma was the disciplinarian, and Papa always left that task to her, so long as he felt she was being fair, and prudent. Mamma always stayed guided by Papa."

"I recall when Papa became ill. It was in winter, when it was cold and raining. Going and coming from work, Papa got soaking wet and caught a cold he couldn't shake despite all he, Mamma, and the doctors did."

"It was a cold January day when Papa left River street trying to get back home again. He just wasn't up to it. He found himself a seat on a nearby park bench when someone who recognized him, telephoned a grocery store near our house. He told my brother John, and my cousin Ephriam, to come to get Papa. They rode on their bicycle to find Papa. They loaded him onto their bicycle and rode him home. In those Great Depression days, taxi services were not available to Black Savannahians."

"My father, Walter Wallie Simmons, was the first child of James and Nellie Moultrie Simmons. He was born in Okatie then known as Okitty, South Carolina."

"It is my understanding that he managed to acquire a fifth grade literacy while helping out on his father's farm. At an early age, he left home to earn more money to help his parents. Somewhere, unknown to any of us, he became a skilled riverboat pilot, and he merited a First Class River Boat Pilot's License (copy in Appendix). I understand he was qualified to take boats from Charleston, S.C. to Jacksonville, Fla."

"Papa worked at a time—when there was no sick days and no unemployment compensation (No work—no pay), and as I've said some time in 1934, Papa became ill, but after a short confinement, he felt threatened: The rent man would put a **for rent sign** on a person's front door. Renters were prone to do just that in those days. Papa returned to work before he was really well enough to do so."

On a cold wintry rainy day, he got wet and became more ill, consequently developing pneumonia.

# 9

# More of Remembering Papa!

## (An Interview by Walter Bruce Simmons and Lou Rivers)

<u>Lou</u>: Walter, tell me more to clear up certain confusions I have.

<u>Walter B</u>: Lou, my sisters and I talked. We are chargin, however at how little we can consciously recall of Papa during his life time with us. We now regret not having observed and recorded more of what he said and did when he was alive.

<u>Lou</u>: Walter, I'm not certain I understand how your brother, John, and your cousin, Ephriam, used their bicycles to ride your sick father home from the park where he'd rested ill coming from work.

<u>Walter B</u>: There was only **one** bicycle. Getting him home again, they balanced him on the one bike. Then they walked as they guided the bike, carefully steering him home.

<u>Lou</u>: Does Ephriam remember anything in particular about this?

<u>Walter B</u>: I will check with him to see if he or anyone else recalls that exact day in the winter of 1934.

<u>Lou</u>: But he died in 1935, you say?

<u>Walter B</u>: Papa was hospitalized soon after they'd brought him home. He died on January 23, 1935, a year later in the Marine Hospital located on York and Abecorn streets. It was a governmental hospital for male patients **only.**

<u>Lou</u>: He died of pneumonia and other complications?

<u>Walter B</u>: We have a copy of his death certificate.

<u>Lou</u>: Perchance he made a deathbed statement?

<u>Walter B</u>: I don't recall anyone saying Papa made any deathbed statement. However, I will check with Bessie and Nellie to be sure.

<u>Lou</u>: Do you remember more details of his funeral?

<u>Walter B</u>: Yes. I can vividly recall his wake, and I will check with others to be certain if anything extraordinary did occur.

<u>Lou</u>: Where was the wake held?

<u>Walter B</u>: Held on a very cold January night at our house.

<u>Lou</u>: Which house? The house on East Broad street?

<u>Walter B</u>: It was the house on East Broad street. I remember it was impossible to get Papa's casket into the house through the front door. The undertakers then took the window sash from the front room window frame and passed Papa's casket through the window into the living room.

I also recall someone had told my brother, Frank, and me that if we rubbed the face of the dead person, we would not be afraid of the dead ever again. When no one was looking, Frank and I lifted the veil on Papa's casket, and we rubbed his face. I was especially struck on feeling how cold his face felt. I don't know about Frank, but I have never known fear again of the dead. As a young adult, I often went on death calls for Williams and Williams Funeral Home, located on Gwinnette street. I also assisted—from time to time within the Williams and Williams' embalming room.

<u>Lou</u>: Was the Williams and Williams' Funeral Home located next door to where the Simmons lived on Gwinnette street?

<u>Walter B</u>: Yes, next door to us.

<u>Lou</u>: Your Father's funeral services were held in Savannah, Ga. at the St. James A.M.E. Church?

<u>Walter B</u>: Yes. Papa's services began in Savannah at St. James A.M.E. Church with Rev. J. Frank Rogers officiating; at the time Reverend Rogers was the church's pastor in charge. He gave Papa's eulogy.

I also remember coming home from East Broad Street School where Juanita and I were in first grade. Mamma placed us both on her lap and explained to us that Papa had died. I was devastated. We went upstairs to cry on our beds.

I heard my sisters talk about an aunt who came often to live with us from time to time, never making contributions, if any, in support of the family. On Papa's death, my sisters reported she was overheard complaining: "What am I going to do? Wallie has gone and left me will all these children." To my sisters, this was a joke they had to report.

<u>Lou</u>: Tell me about Ephriam and Alma.

<u>Walter B</u>: I'm not sure of the date Ephriam came to live with us, but it seems he was always there! Same thing with Alma. Our Mother, an extraordinary woman, born to "mother" everyone she thought needed "mothering." Ephriam's mother was our Mother's oldest sister's child. She was Louise Simmons Alston. Ephriam's father was Richard Alston. Together they had six children—Clifford, Edward, Janie, Cornelia, Paul, and Ephriam. Clifford was the oldest and Paul was the youngest. I'm not sure how they lined up by age, but I have learned that upon Louise's death, Richard remarried. This stepmother was mean to the children, and someone told our mother heard about it, and Mamma walked from 518 East Oglethorpe Avenue to West Savannah, quite a distance, to confront the mean stepmother. After more of these confrontations, Mamma bought the Alston children home to live with us, and the Alston children lived with us until they were able to take care of themselves. One by one, they moved away. Ephriam was the last to leave. He stayed until he married Lucille Singleton and they began a family of their own.

<u>Lou</u>: And Alma? What about her?

<u>Walter B</u>: Alma is the daughter of Mamma's brother, Frank Simmons and his wife Ida.

Frank and Ida always quarreled, and consequently they separated. Uncle Frankee as we called him usually brought Alma to Mamma. When he and Ida got together again, he would take Alma back with him and Ida.

However, I'm told, that on one occasion, while they were separating again, someone dropped Alma off at the corner of Price Street and Oglethorpe Avenue. Alma was not yet six years old. Nonetheless, she came running all the way to the house with only the clothes she had on her back. She never left us again, not until she married Edward Campbell in 1942. Remember now Mamma's maiden surname was Simmons. She married Papa whose surname was also Simmons. Alma was a Simmons and as she grew, she was considered to be more than a cousin. She was always a sister.

# Part Two

**The Sun Beams
On
The Simmons Family**

Daisy Alice Simmons, Matriarch

# Daisy Takes Control

Wallie,
        I love you.
In so many different
ways!

I love you for each of
    our eight children.

And I will go on loving
    you, Wallie, even
beyond the last Sunset.

Alice's Apostrophes *
contiue

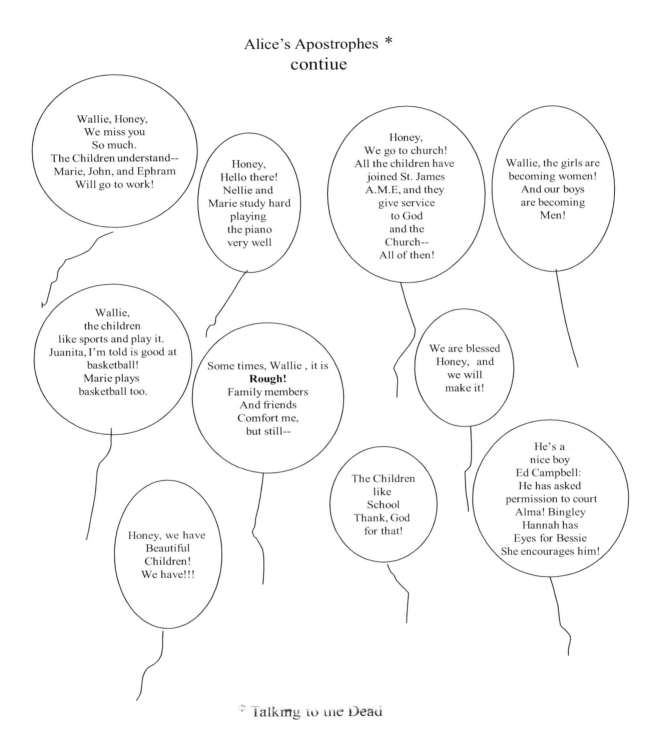

Wallie, Honey,
We miss you
So much.
The Children understand--
Marie, John, and Ephram
Will go to work!

Honey,
Hello there!
Nellie and
Marie study hard
playing
the piano
very well

Honey,
We go to church!
All the children have
joined St. James
A.M.E, and they
give service
to God
and the
Church--
All of then!

Wallie, the girls are
becoming women!
And our boys
are becoming
Men!

Wallie,
the children
like sports and play it.
Juanita, I'm told is good at
basketball!
Marie plays
basketball too.

Some times, Wallie , it is
**Rough!**
Family members
And friends
Comfort me,
but still--

We are blessed
Honey,  and
we will
make it!

He's a
nice boy
Ed Campbell:
He has asked
permission to court
Alma! Bingley
Hannah has
Eyes for Bessie
She encourages him!

Honey, we have
Beautiful
Children!
We have!!!

The Children
like
School
Thank, God
for that!

* Talking to the Dead

27

Alice's Apostrophes

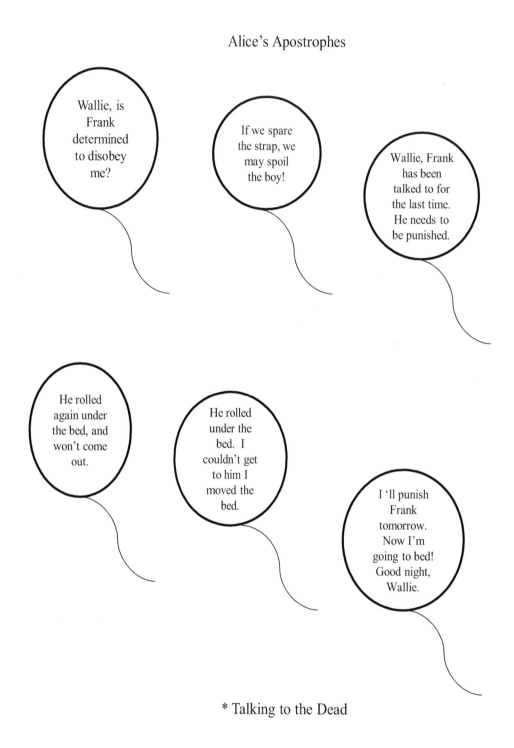

* Talking to the Dead

More of Alice's Apostrophes *

337 East Broad Street becomes a radio listening station! When Joe Louis fights, The children's friends and neighbors gather to listen to the radio. Joe Louis is our hero!

Many of our relatives come and go. Some stay longer than others. They go to school here. As you know, there aren't any high schools for African-American children in Bluffton, South Carolina.

We have always been short of beds, but our children don't mind sleeping on pallets when company comes. They use blankets they make into beds they place on the floors. They think it's fun and it's funny, honey.

Mamma received many thanks for my generous hostility.

I'm all right. I broke my wrist climbing up onto the back of the truck taking me and others to work.

I took a job, Wallie. It is being a seamstress to sew mattress covers for armed services

* Talking to the Dead

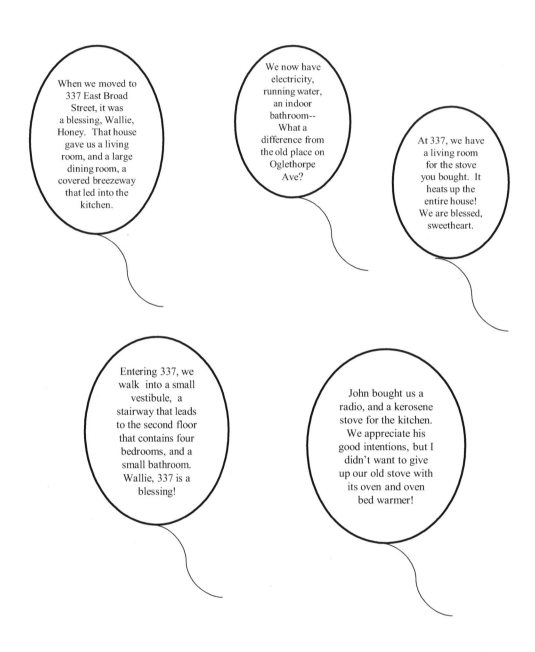

When we moved to 337 East Broad Street, it was a blessing, Wallie, Honey. That house gave us a living room, and a large dining room, a covered breezeway that led into the kitchen.

We now have electricity, running water, an indoor bathroom-- What a difference from the old place on Oglethorpe Ave?

At 337, we have a living room for the stove you bought. It heats up the entire house! We are blessed, sweetheart.

Entering 337, we walk into a small vestibule, a stairway that leads to the second floor that contains four bedrooms, and a small bathroom. Wallie, 337 is a blessing!

John bought us a radio, and a kerosene stove for the kitchen. We appreciate his good intentions, but I didn't want to give up our old stove with its oven and oven bed warmer!

\* Talking to the Dead

More of Alice's Apostophes*

337 is a very popular place, Wallie! Every day and night it is an important house for many!

Our children, all of them, show love and care and a share attitude! Thank God for that. And for you too, Wallie, thank God for that!

In the living room our children and their friends play the piano! They are learning and singing the latest popular songs

Our children and friends gather on cold days and evenings around the oval heater in the dinning room.

At a certain hour in the evening I declare the last piece of coal for the fire. That means it is time for all friends to go home

* Talking to the Dead

Wallie, our children understand so much. They don't whine: they go to work; John, so does Ephriam and Marie-- We have good children!

They understand going to work doesn't mean they won't go to school! They must all finish school! Those who work will go to Adult Night School. They all must finish school! They must!

They will play sports too.

John, Ephriam, Walter and Frank have to chop wood, collect the wood and stack if for use in the kitchen. Each girl has her chores to do too.

And they know they must all go to church too, Wallie, I'll see to that. You know I will!

\* Talking to the Dead

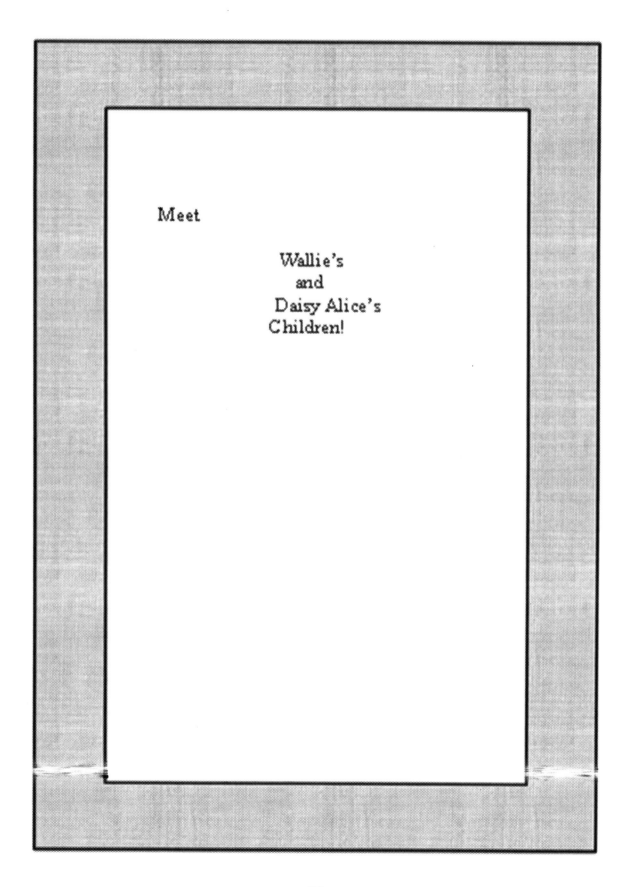

Meet

Wallie's
and
Daisy Alice's
Children!

We are six sisters

We were *six* Sisters:

Marie
Nellie
Bessie
Alma (Cousin)
Eugenia
 and
Juanita

## I am Marie "Big Sister"

•I am Marie Simmons Kennedy, Walllie's and Daisy Simmons' first born.

• I was born on March 4, 1910 in Bluffon, S.C.

• We moved to Savannah, Ga., when Papa became pilot of Island Girl, a riverboat.

•I attended Savannah public schools and graduated from the old Beach High School located on Price and Harris streets.

•I also studied at Savannah's Vocational School earning a certificate in Home Economics

•I was considered an excellent steamstress and a "damn good cook". Ask my family about my bread puddings and fruitcakes.

•I learned to play the piano Papa bought for me. I played for both churches and social club gatherings

• At a young age, I joined and served St. James A.M.E. Church.

•I first married Wesley Fabian who died early in our marriage.

•Then I married Hemmer Kennedy.

•I had no children by either marriage.

•Instead, I embraced more of my loving family who doubling returned love to me; all the love I gave to them, and I loved them completely; they made life more beautiful for me.

•**On August 17, 1994 I returned in death to meet Mamma, Papa, and other loved ones.**

I am Nellie, "the Adorable One"

•I am Nellie Elizabeth Simmons Oxner ,Wallie's and Daisy Alice's second daughter.

•I was born in Bluffton, S.C. on August 23, 1916

•I was 3 years old when we moved to Savannah, Ga.

•I attended Savannah's public schools . I attended East Broad Street Elementary School, Beach-Cuyler Jr. High School and Beach Cuyler Senior High School.

•I attended Georgia State College (Now Savannah State University) I majored in Home Economics.

•I remained an honor student throughout my school career.

•I graduated from Georgia State College in 1939.

•While in college I did not participate in co-curricular activities. Instead I worked in the Office of a federally funded program (The NYA)

•I did post graduate studies at Johnson C. Smith University. I earned a teacher's certificate.

•I also studied at Columbia University where I received a Master's Degree in Elementary Education

•While living in Savannah, I remained an active member in St. James A.M.E. Church. I served as Organist for the Sunday School and the Senior Choir

•When I graduated from Georgia State College in 1939 . I began my teaching career that started in Savannah, Ga and ended in Bainbridge Ga. in 1943.

•For a period , I worked with the Federal Security Agency in Washington D.C. I worked as a statistical verifier

•In 1949, I married Jerome Oxner and moved with him to Charlotte, North Carolina

•In North Carolina I renewed teaching credentials , elementary education at Johnson C. Smith University

•Jerome and I had no children

•The Jane Ford and Frank Simmons Family Reunion Association awarded me its first <u>Educational Pioneer Award</u> at the family's 2005 Reunion. I was the first in the family to graduate from high school and to receive a college degree.

•In my lifetime, I have been the recipient of numerous Civic and Church awards and citations.

•In Charlotte, N.C., I became an active and supportive member of Grace A.M.E. Zion Church

•I've served as Program Director, organist for the Bible Study Program, chairperson and Greeter for the Church's Birthday Program

•I served on the Board of Directors of the North Carolina Illiteracy Association for more than eleven years. I have served as volunteer tutor, teaching reading to adults.

•I've supported many local charities in the Charlotte North Carolina area.

•I continued to be a supporter of St. James, A.M.E. Church in Savannah, Ga. and the Frank Callen Boys' and Girls' Club in Savannah, Ga.

•My family tell me I continue to grow in grace, patience, empathy, charity and style.

•**Nellie Elizabeth Simmons Oxner died on Friday, August 27. 2010 after a short illness.**

"Some people know the way to make each day seem more worthwhile.

They do the nicest things for you and always wear a smile.

They make this world a better place by practicing the art of reaching out to others and by giving from the heart. That was Nellie."

"Some people know the way to make each day seem more worthwhile.

They do the nicest things for you and always wear a smile.

They make this world a better place by practicing the art of reaching out to others and by giving from the heart. That was Nellie."

"Dear Family and Friends,

"We thank you with all of our hearts, for the loving and generous support which you have given us, as we grieved for an Angel, Nellie Elizabeth Simmons Oxner.

"We dutifully noted your many and varied expressions of love and support.

"You have shown yourself to be a person of great good will!

"It was especially heart warming to have so many coming to Savannah to help us bear up at this time.

"Please accept this as an expression of sincere love and appreciation.

"With warm and loving affections,

The Simmons Family"

I am Bessie, "The Bossy One"

•I am Bessie Gertruide Simmons Hannah, Wallie's and Dasiy's fourth child, third daughter

•I was born on November 12, 1918 in Bluffton, S.C.

•When I was 2 years old, our family moved to Savannah, Ga.

•I attended East Broad Street Elementary Public School. I then attended and graduated from Beach-Cuyler Junior and Senior High Schools.

•In high schools, I played guardian on the school's basketball teams.

•I graduated high school in June 1937.

•In high schools, I sang in the Glee Clubs, and acted in the drama club

•I attended Georgia State College (now Savannah State University ) I graduated with a B.S. in Education

•I then attended Atlanta University in Atlanta, Ga.

•My high school sweet heart, Bingley Hannah and I got married and we had two boys, Bingley Hannah II and Frank S. Hannah.

**•My faithful husband, endearing sweetheart, died on October 10, 2006.**

# Walter Bruce's Comments on Bessie

• Bessie was always the big sister. Frank, my brother, and I found her "bossy" where we were concerned. She always insisted we bathe– frequently-- and change clothing, especially our under clothing. Several times, she would say to me when I was about to go on a date-- "Did you wash under your arms?" Then she would pull me closer to her so she could actually smell me. Then she would say "Shame on you! Going to see a girl, and you haven't washed."

•When B.S. Hannah asked Mamma if he could marry Bessie, Mamma's reply was "You never asked if you could come to court her"!

•I also recalled when B.S. was courting Bessie, he and "Dump" Nathaniel Noble, were at the same time pursuing Bessie. "Dump" went to the U.S. Navy leaving open the courting of Bessie. There was one other suitor coming from out of town. When B.S. found out, he got some bigger guys on the block (East Broad & Gwinnett Sts.) to intimidate that suitor to the extent he never returned, and I think B.S. discouraged all other suitors, because I can't recall any other suitor other than he.

•I do, however, remember when my sisters were courting, the courting time had to end at a certain time. My mother would yell from upstairs "Don't put any more of my wood or coals on the fire!"

•I don't recall much about Bessie's high school days, other than her playing basketball for Beach and me wearing her sneakers, unbeknown to her.

•After graduating from college, Bessie found a teaching job in Cuthbert, Ga. The unique factor was the principal of the school was Fletcher Henderson's father. Fletcher would bring his band to the school every year to raise funds for the school.

•After Cuthbert, Bessie moved on to Douglas, Georgia. B.S.'s Aunt was an esteemed teacher there and her husband was a mover and shaker in the community.

•Other times she might yell from upstairs "Bring me my clock!" That was a signal indicating it was time for B.S. to go home. B.S. was resourceful. Often he would bring some wood or coals with him, and he was known to "reset" the clock to an earlier hour before it was handed to my mother.

•When Mamma could not be at home to cook, because of employment, Marie, Nellie, or Bessie took turns to prepare the family's meals. That's when I learned to eat hurriedly. All eight or nine of us would sit around the big round dining table. When Bessie prepared the meal, she would serve it around the table, serving each person's plate. The problem was, Bessie some times experienced the problem of not having cooked enough. Frequently, she would have to go back around the table to take back from each plate in order to have enough to go around. After a while, Frank and I learned to take no chances! We ate quickly whatever she placed on our plates.

•Bessie and Bingley did not have a lot of money to give to the family to help siblings. Bessie, however gave generously and freely her time, talents and care whenever she saw the need to give. We never had to ask Bessie for a favor; if she saw any of us in need she voluntarily did what she saw needed to be done.

•When she was on leave, or during the summer months, she came and cared for me or my children, while Mary, my wife, went to work. Our children loved to be with their Aunt Bessie.

•Finally as a result of much prayers by Mamma, Bessie and Jeannie were offered teaching positions at home and my wife Mary, were able to become beginning teachers in Savannah.  At that time, I had become a volunteer at the Frank Callen Boys' Club. Mr. Callen, founder of the club, had passed on by that time, and his wife Erma was running the Boys' Club. Erma's sister, Rosemary, was a supervisor in the local school system and had considerable influence with W.C. McCune, who at that time ran the personnel department. Mamma is reported to have persuaded Rosemary, (Mrs. Rosemary Curley Jackson) to make it possible for her children to get work as teachers at home.

•Rosemary told Mamma to have the girls apply using her, Rosemary, as reference.  Bessie, Jeanie and my wife, Mary received interviews and consequently were hired in 1951 as teachers in Savannah's School system.

I am Alma Marie, "Cousin-Sister"

• I am Alma Marie Simmons Campbell

• I was born on February 21, 1921 in Savannah, Ga.

•I am first cousin to Marie, Nellie and other Simmons children.

•I was the elder of two children born to Mr. and Mrs. Frank Simmons who was Daisy Alice's brother.

•Because of a separation of my parents when I was five years old, my father gave me to his sister to be raised.

•I was raised in the Simmons' home as if I were one of the sisters.

•I moved from the Simmons' house when I married Edward Campbell of Savannah, Ga.

•Because my last name was Simmons, most folks assumed I was a sister

•Growing up in the Simmons house, I never saw nor felt any situation when I was treated less than a sister.

•I followed the traditional family's trail of schooling. I attended East Broad Street Elementary school, Cuyler Junior High Scool

•I graduated Cuyler Beach high school, June 1940.

•In school, I participated in the Glee and Dramatic clubs. I was an exceptionally good dancer and was a popular dance partner.

• I was also a varsity Cheerleader

•I also joined St. James A.M.E. Church under the pastorate of the late Rev. Frank Rogers

• Under Rev. Frank Rogers ' leadership I stayed actively involved in Youth Activities, Sunday School, A.C.E. League, Junior Choir, Junior and Senior Usher Boards.

•Upon graduating from high school, I selected to make Beauty Culture my chosen field of work. I attended and graduated from Madam Cargo's School of Beauty Culture

•During World War II, I married Edward B. Campbell. During our high school years, we had become a romantic duo in Savannah

• Ed and I gave life to two girls

•Our first daughter died in infancy.

•Our second daughter, Eugenia, named in honor of Eugenia, my sister– cousin. She died at the age of 35, the mother of four beautiful children .

•**My precious life came to an end in February 1960.**

I am Eugenia, "the Patient One"

• I am Eugenia Simmons Durden Glover, Walter's and Daisy Alice's sixth child. They all called me "Jeannie" the patient one.

• Wallie and Alice trained us all to be good American citizens

•And we all became life long active members of St. James A.M.E. Church

•During the past 65 years, I have served in the church in the following capacities:

•Exhorter, Steward, Missionary, Stewardess, Sunday School Teacher, Vacation School Teacher, Pastor's Aid, Board Advisor, YPD Teacher, Senior Citizens Ministry and in other activities .

•I attended East Broad St. Elementary School in Savannah, Ga.

•I graduated from Beach Cuyler High School in Savannah, Ga. It was in 1940.

•I then attended Georgia State College, now Savannah State University

•After receiving my B.S. degree, I studied to receive a Master's degree in Early Childhood Development, a Certificate in Teaching Reading.

•For my activities to teach reading on all levels, I was selected to teach under Title I (a federal sponsored program)

•After 35 years of teaching, I retired in 1985. However, in my career I was chosen and celebrated as "Teacher of the Year." I received plaques and citations.

•I have been enshrined in the A.E. Beach High School's Athletic Hall of Fame

•I am a member of Alpha Zeta Sorority Kappa Honor Society in Education

•I am also a member in the Elegant Ladies Social and Civic Club, the Frank Callen Boys' and Girls' Club

•I am a member of the Savannah Chatham Country Retired Teachers Organization

•My brothers, sisters, cousins, and I grew up on the East side of Savannah, Ga. called the Old Fort.

•In the Old Fort, we were lucky to have lived near Crawford Square where there were sports activities. However, I must say we girls realized so many of the sports opportunities and activities favored boys.

•Crawford Square had limited equipments and opportunities but, we were creative.

•We made the roots of pulled up grass to serve as play hair we braided.

•We made balls from wads of old newspapers and strings

•We turned old broom handles into bats, peach kernels and shells into jackstones. We cut small rubber balls into halves to play "half rubber".

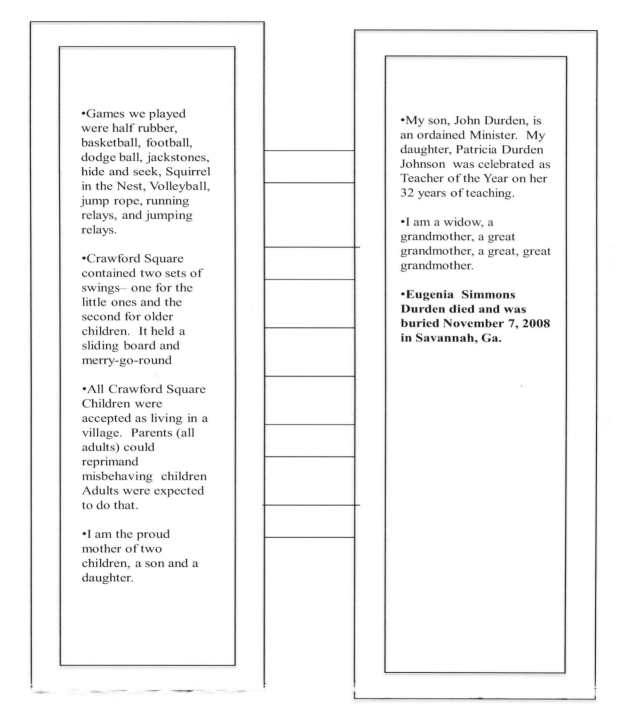

•Games we played were half rubber, basketball, football, dodge ball, jackstones, hide and seek, Squirrel in the Nest, Volleyball, jump rope, running relays, and jumping relays.

•Crawford Square contained two sets of swings– one for the little ones and the second for older children. It held a sliding board and merry-go-round

•All Crawford Square Children were accepted as living in a village. Parents (all adults) could reprimand misbehaving children Adults were expected to do that.

•I am the proud mother of two children, a son and a daughter.

•My son, John Durden, is an ordained Minister. My daughter, Patricia Durden Johnson was celebrated as Teacher of the Year on her 32 years of teaching.

•I am a widow, a grandmother, a great grandmother, a great, great grandmother.

•**Eugenia Simmons Durden died and was buried November 7, 2008 in Savannah, Ga.**

I'm Juanita, "the Organizer"

•I am Juanita Simmons Marks. I am Wallie's and Daisy's youngest daughter. I am the sixth girl following my Cousin Alma and sister Eugenia. Alma was my first cousin, but more like a sister.

•I was born August 17, 1928.

•**My beautiful and peaceful life came to an end on earth on August 14, 1988.**

•I rest in Magnolia Memorial Garden Cemetery in Savannah Georgia.

•I attended and finished the following Savannah schools– East Broad Street Elementary School, Beach Cuyler Jr. High School, and Beach Cuyler Senior High School

•Throughout my school career, I remained an outstanding student

•At East Broad Street Elementary School I was in earliest grades but selected to read to upper level students.

•In high school, I was active in most student affairs. I sang with the school's concert choir and glee club.

•I was an active member in the Dramatic Club. I was a Varsity Cheerleader and Varsity basketball player.

•I have been enshrined into the Beach High School Athletic Hall of Fame, and I served in the Student Governments.

• My friends say I was blessed to have a warm and pleasing personality.

•I was president of the popular club, the Demoiselles. I took members aside, one-on-one, and taught them the intricacies of the two-step, the jitterbug, and the waltz. The Demoiselles placed time and attention on stylish dressing and conventions of polite society.

•I received many citations for my many socio/civic and religious contributions.

•I attended and graduated from Georgia State College, now Savannah State University.

•I taught English at Midway Junior High School in Midway, Ga.

•In 1950, I received an MA in Supervision and Administration from Hunter College in New York City.

•I married Earl Dexter, Marks of Savannah, Ga.

•We had three children. Dr. Earl Dexter Mark Jr., Phillip Marks and Regina Alice Marks.

•Dexter has two children, Phillip has three, and Regina has three children.

•I returned to live in Savannah, Ga., and to rejoin my family 's church, Saint James A.M.E. Church., and I served the church in many areas.

•Did I mention my son, Dr. Earl Dexter Jr. served as an interpreter for the United Nations? He had also served as a teacher.

•My son, Phillip, is in Auto body works. He returned to live in Savannah.

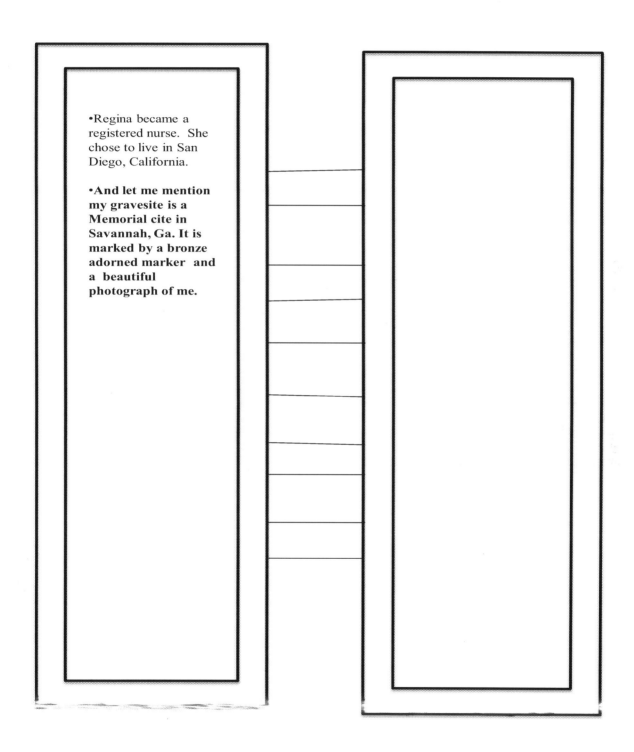

•Regina became a registered nurse. She chose to live in San Diego, California.

**•And let me mention my gravesite is a Memorial cite in Savannah, Ga. It is marked by a bronze adorned marker and a beautiful photograph of me.**

**We Were Four Brothers:**
**John**
**Ephriam  (first cousin)**
**Frank**
**and**
**Walter Bruce**

I am John

**(John Augustus Simmons**
by Jeannie S. Glover & Walter B. Simmons

•The second child and first son born to Wallie and Alice was John Augustus Simmons. He was born in Bluffton, South Carolina on June 14, 1914.

•The family moved to Savannah, Georgia when John was five years old. John may have been the most scholastic and talented of his siblings. He was able to assist Marie, his older sister, in her school work. She would say to John, "I don't understand this problem. And John would look the situation over and very soon say, "Big Sis, it tells you exactly what to do, right here" Marie would retort, "It might tell you; it doesn't tell me anything!" John would then show Marie what she'd not understood before.

•John taught himself to play the piano by notes. He also taught himself to play guitar. He could sing all voices and all parts of a song. He sang with the "Famous Simmons Singers of Savannah" and while in Merchant Marines, the Army, he sang with the famous "Singing Sergeants".

•Count Basie's band played at the Savannah City Auditorium during the late 1930's. As was customary during those times, a local talent was allowed to sing on stage along with the band. During this time, John had cultivated an outstanding rendition of "Danny Boy" accompanied by Nellie, his second sister. So John sang, "Danny Boy", unrehearsed with Count Basie's Band. During those days, Basie's vocalist was "Little Jimmie Rushing", who specialized in singling the Blues. (We imagine John would have been tried out on ballards and love songs) Unfortunately, Mamma would not agree for John to take the offer. She was afraid of "fast life" she had heard musicians loved. Besides, Papa had just died, and this was the height of the Great Depression and John, at that time, was a major supporter of the family. Always as most obedient son, John passed up on the Count Basie's offer.

•John proved to be most reliable, supportive and dedicated. He was our "big brother." So much so, his peers called him "Sis Boom". We never heard what that meant. A story is told that when John was still a kid, he wanted to go down in the "Old field" of the Old Fort to fly his kite. Mamma instructed him to stay in the backyard and "don't go out through the gate." Later, John and his kite were missing: He was discovered down in Jones Old Field flying his kite."

•Upon his return home, Mamma immediately challenged him with, "John, I told you Not To Go Not To Go Out of That Gate"! His reply was "Yes Mam, I know, that's why I went over the fence"! We are told he escaped punishment that day.

•John followed the established educational trail of East Broad Street Elementary School, Cuyler Junior High and Beach Senior High. John, always an honor student, was allowed to drop out of daytime school to go to work full time after Mamma suffered a broken arm and could not work.

•We are told John was always a bright pupil, and he always came in second or third honors during his elementary school days. This was because he would frequently be late in completing his assignments. We are told whenever he detected what might be an error, rather than erase, he would do the complete work all over again. He wanted his work to be right and neat.

•His trend-to be late in completing his assignments continued in high school as his classmates bugged him for correct answers and for opportunities to copy from his papers.

•During his high school days, John found employment after school. Somewhere among our family artifacts is a certificate declaring him to be a golf caddy for the Savannah Golf Course Club.

•At an early adolescent age, John worked as a presser in a dry cleaning establishment. Lifting heavy pressing irons, he developed a problem with his back that caused him to lean slightly to one side. After Papa died, Uncle Frank, Mamma's brother, got John and Ephriam hired as warehouse workers for Haverty's Furniture store. Later John was able to secure a job in the Savannah Public School System as an assistant custodian at Beach-Cuyler High School. At this time, John acted as the unofficial basketball coach of the varsity team. Most of the boys on the varsity teams at Beach were from Crawford Square or the Old Fort. The teams would practice immediately after school. The basketball teams practiced on the campus; the football team walked to Cann Park at 45th and Stevens Street to practice. This was before days of free lunches. Most of these boys and girls were at school all day with no lunch or time or convenience to commute home for food, between school time and practice time. We were told by our brother Frank and other players that John often served them "after school snacks." We never heard nor tried to find out how he was able to afford this.

•We are told Mamma never knew nor pretended to know instead of Frank going to work, he was playing varsity sports. She was led to believe Frank had an after school job. John would, somehow, provide Frank some money to give to Mamma from time to time. (Frank was a Savannah Morning News Carrier all through high school)

John worked as the custodian at Harris Street School. While John was working at Harris Street school Mamma had me, Walter, to go there in the afternoons to assist him. I can recall cleaning the ashes out of those pot belly heaters and setting them for the mornings by placing them with paper, kindling wood and coals on the grate. The next morning, John had only to strike a match to each pot belly stove to get the day's fire going.

During this time, we were impressed as we noticed the young female teachers, doing what we thought to be flirting with our big brother, the janitor! During this time, John was courting Estelle Doby. She would frequently visit John in the evenings while he was cleaning the class rooms. We recall two of them making beautiful music as they sang together the popular songs of the day.

•Some time later in the early 1940's, John took an examination for a job with the U.S. Maritime Service. He passed the test with distinction and was assigned to a dredge that served the Savannah Harbor. Shortly after securing this job, John's draft status was changed to 1A, and he was drafted. We were told that he made such an impression with his work on the dredge that he was guaranteed a job, once his military service was over.

•John had had a romance with Mary Beaton. We don't know what happened to that affair, but years later, she talked to Walter, with fondness for John.

•John and Estella Doby married before he was inducted into the Merchant Marines.

• John and Estella had no children

• **John died_ November 4, 1944 serving his country**

•**He is buried in Lincoln Memorial Cemetery, Savannah, GA**

**Estella died June 8, 2011**

I am Ephriam Alston, Cousin-Brother

•I am Ephriam Lucious Alston.

•I was born on April 7, 1914 in Bluffton, South Carolina to Richard Alston and Louise Simmons Alston.

•After the death of my parents, I was accepted as a Simmons  brother by my cousins, who lived in Savannah, Georgia.

•After graduating from high school, I went to New York to live with my siblings, Janie Strobert, Paul Alston, Eddie Alston, and Corenelia Pierce.

•I then went to Cincinnati to visit and live for a short time with my brother, Clifford Alston.

•I met Lucille Singleton, my wife of 67 years, through a friend, Lawrence Bird.  We have three children: Ann, Charles, and Kay; six grandchildren: Cecille, Camille, Richard Bolton IV, and Charles Clifford Jr., Bruck and Whitney Anne Alston.

• When a young man, I worked at the *Savannah Morning and Evening Newspaper* Building on Bay Street while attending Georgia State College (now Savannah State University.)

• Later I began a career with aircraft  at the  Hunter Army Base.

•Later I found a more lucrative career as an Aerospace Supervisor of Aircraft and Machinery at Warner Robins Air Base for the remainder of my career. I was one of the first Black supervisors in Aircraft which required merit travel to many countries, including Thailand, the Phillipine, Chuanute, and Illinois where I taught both military and civilian workers.

•Shortly after retirement., I lived in Atlanta with my wife and family.

•I became a member of Saint James A.M.E. Church in Savannah Georgia where I sang in the choir and served as a Steward and Trustee.

•Among my favorite songs were "O Come All Ye Faithfuls", "I Must Tell Jesus", "He Touched Me", and "The Lord's Prayer". The church recognized me for my many good works.

•I made friends with everyone I met. I was a quiet spoken man with great courage. I found God early in my life and I understood as I lived the true purpose that God wanted all of us, his children, to fulfill. My special love was my blood family and extended family, with whom my ties were always steadfast. My family and extended family, with whom my ties were always steadfast.

•My wisdom came from my spiritual experiences. My favorite **Biblical** thoughts were "Do unto others, as you would have them do unto you and Love thy neighbor".

• **I lived to cherish my loving wife, Lucille Singleton Alston; our daughters, Ann Alston and Kay Alston Bolton (Richard Bolton, III); and my son, Charles C. Alston; grandchildren-- Cecille Bolton, Camille Bolton, Richard Bolton IV, Charles C. Alston Jr., Bruce Alston, and Whitney and Alston.**

### A Word on Ephriam Alston
### **By Walter Bruce Simmons**

• Ephriam's mother , Louise Simmons Alston, was married to Richard Alston.

•Louise died early, leaving the following children: Clifford, Eddie, Cornelia, Janie, Ephriam, and Paul.

•Richard eventually remarried.  The children would then come to my mom who complained of abuse by their step mother.

•On one occasion in 1930, after Paul and Ephriam had walked from their  home in West Savannah to complain about abuses,  Mamma stopped washing clothes,  took the boys back to West Savannah, gathered what few belongings they possessed and brought them home with her to stay.

• Paul  soon went also to live with his older brother Eddie in New York.  The other siblings had already gone to live in New York.

•Ephriam remained with us until he married Lucille Singleton.

• Ephriam  and Lucille had three children.  Anne and Kaye are teachers in Atlanta.  Charles is a physician in Chicago.

I am Frank Edwards Simmons, " A Star"

**Frank Was Truly The Family's Star**
By Walter Bruce Simmons

•Frank Edward Simmons was Wallie's and Alice Simmons' second son. He was the first born after the family moved to Savannah, Georgia from Bluffton, S.C.

•Frank came into the world on East Boundary Street in 1921. After Frank's birth, the family moved to 518 East Oglethorpe Avenue.

•He was named for his mother's brother, Frank and his father's brother, Edward.

•Crawford Square was situated within three blocks of where he lived and very early in life, Frank found Crawford Square to be an oasis.

•Frank followed the established public school trail of East Broad Street Elementary School and then Beach Cuyler, junior an senior high schools.

•He succeeded Joe Greene as Athletic Director and football coach at Beach High School. During this time, he was instrumental in having varsity baseball implemented as a sport at Beach, Tompkins, and Johnson, Black High Schools.

•He introduced tennis and golf to the curriculum at Beach High School.

•Frank entered the Korean War as a Second Lieutenant, and was discharged a Captain.

•According to Walter, Frank's brother, one of the proudest moments in his life was to have Frank and Edward Campbell watching as his Beach High Basketball team won the Georgia State Championship in 1946.

•Frank "saved me" from drowning at one time says Walter. At some time during the mid 1930's, Frank took Walter to the recently opened swimming pool at 39th and Ogeechee Road. "I was floating on a raft with a bunch of boys and got pushed off the raft. The raft moved on and left me struggling to get to the top and to remain at the top. Just when I figured I had given my all and I was ready to give up the struggle to survive, somebody grabbed me! To my great relief, it was Frank. Immediately following this incident, the pool's monitor wanted me to get my clothes. In his checking, he realized we had paid only one fare rather than two. After the excitement, however had cooled, we checked out without our scheme being revealed".

•As a teenager, Frank would often take naps. His friends would come by to get him to go "play some ball" somewhere. His job however, was to keep enough wood chopped for the day. When his friends came by to get him, and he had to chop wood, however, in order to expedite time would have his friends prepared to help him chop wood. They would chop an abundance of wood! The only problem was – it was my job, Walter's to bring in the wood, and I had no help!

•John and Ephriam, graciously, allowed Frank to share in the few dress clothing that they had. Only problem, Frank could not afford to open his coat. He had to have the long legged-for him-pants pulled up to his chest.

•One summer they all wanted to forget is when Frank, Campbell and some other boys from Savannah, were in Baltimore trying to "catch a ship". They were having a difficult time. James "Jimmy" Drayton, extended an invitation to take them out to dinner. They went to a restaurant, about five, all together. When the meal was just about finished, Drayton instructed one, then another, then another to leave the restaurant. Soon it was just Drayton and Frank eating at the table. When they looked up, there was the chef standing over them with a hatchet and his hands folded across his chest. On some kind of signal, Drayton suddenly knocked over the table, Frank put a football hit on the chef and they were all out of there!

•During the 1960's, Frank was in charge of the city's swimming pool. He taught Life Saving, swimming, and he supervised the pool. During this time, he would take kids to the pool, making them all swimmers.

•Many times I have met former athletic foes of Frank. They always start off with what a great guy he was personally, but—he was a terror and a nightmare on the athletic field.

•Frank graduated from Tuskegee in 1951, with a B.S. degree in Health and Physical Education and a commission as a Second Lieutenant in the U.S. Army.

•During his term at "Skeegee", Frank proved to be an outstanding personality and a great athlete.

•Frank was also very popular with his teammates, fellow students, faculty, and the entire Tuskegee community.

•Frank earned varsity status in football, baseball, basketball and track & field. He also participated in tennis and golf. (Savannah had offered no chance for experience for Blacks in Golf, Tennis or Track & Field at that time.)

•As a 9th grader, Frank earned a starters position on Beach High School's basketball and football teams.

•Frank earned recognition as "All Southern" at this tournament.

•Frank's high school tenure was interrupted by his military service. He enlisted into the U.S. Marines. He was among the first Blacks to be allowed to enlist.

•He received his training at Montford Point, N. C. with several other Savannahians, including Fred Wright, Julius Williams, Soloman Bynes and Fred Owens.

•Frank served a stint as an assistant football coach at Savannah State. He officiated athletics on both high school and collegiate levels. It was impressive to see him move on the athletic field with such agility and grace with his portly physique.

•Frank was a dedicated officer and member of St. James A.M.E. Church. He was a member of the Board of Stewards, President of the A.B. Wilson Male Choir, Bass soloist for the Wilson Choir and the Senior choir.

•He was active with Sunday School, the Laymen organization and Hospitality Club. He became known at church as the "Candy man" because of his habit of bringing candy to church and passing it out among adults and children, alike.

He was active with Sunday School, the Laymen organization and Hospitality Club. He became known at church as the "Candy man" because of his habit of bringing candy to church and passing it out among adults and children alike.

Frank led the family's caravan of three or four cars on the annual summer trips to Disney World, Six Flags, Tuskegee or New York. Frank's car, usually a big red or maroon Lincoln Town Car, was known as the "Chuck wagon" because it was always loaded with "goodies".

On over night stops we would have several rooms and a suite for Frank. Frank would cook meals in his suite.

Frank never smoked nor drank hard drinks, but he always provided quality and bountiful drinks for all of the family affairs.

Frank had many hobbies: photography, Record collecting of Country & Western music, Big Bands, Movies and Dancing. He was an exceptional dancer, in spite of his portly build.

Frank loved to cook. Edward Campbell, Robert "Sunny" Washington were also great cooks. So much, so they often prepared major meals for their families.

•I remember when Frank would come home at night, presumably ready to go to bed, when the whole household was presumably asleep, Frank would quietly sneak down stairs (we all slept up stairs) to prepare himself a steak or some other dish with all the trimmings. Soon his sisters caught on and would come down just in time for the meal. Juanita and I, however, missed out on those midnight escapades.

•Mamma would punish Frank when she thought he misbehaved. It might be better to say, she tried hard to whip him, before he would wind himself up into her apron. She had a time untangling him. He would then roll himself under the bed. She would move the bed, but he would roll with the bed, into the bed's new position. After a while, Mamma would give up from fatigue.

•Then Mamma came up with the idea of having Uncle Frankie (Alma's dad) put a dress on Frank. That proved to be a deterrent for his running off to Crawford Square or some other place away from home. That seemed to work. He would never venture out of the house when he had a dress on. Later to keep me from going out and away from home, they also tried that same trick on me.

•Frank was a great CB communicator and he loved communicating over the CB radio. His CB handle was "Fat Cat".

•Frank has been enshrined into celebrated halls of fame. The first class of the Beach High Athletic Hall of Fame in 1988 and The Greater Savannah Athletic Hall of Fame in 1976 and the Tuskegee University Hall of fame in 1993.

**Frank died in 1990 and is buried in Savannah, Ga.**

I am Walter Bruce Simmons, "Superstar"

Walter B. Simmons is the 3rd and youngest blood son of Wallace and Daisy Alice Simmons! He was born October 29, 1926 in Savannah, Georgia.

Walter matriculated through the local public schools of Savannah. He attended East Broad Street Elementary School, Cuyler Junior High School, and Bach Senior High School.

After a tour in the United States Navy and an honorable discharge, he enrolled in and graduated from Savannah State College with a BS degree in General Science.

The Masters Degree in School Administration he earned at Tuskegee Institute.

At a very early age, he joined the Savannah Boys' Club. For more than fifty years, he has served as member, teen leader, coach, tutorial teacher, interim executive director, and board member.

During his time, he has introduced various recreational activities, instituted intramural sports, organized youth sports leagues in baseball and basketball that provided supervised organized sports, organized youth sports leagues in baseball and basketball that provided supervised organized sport programs for boys of the city.

A varsity basketball program was instituted. This made it possible for boys attending school and having to work after school an opportunity to experience varsity basketball.

We were lovebirds, Walter and Mary

A Post season basketball tournament was initiated. This tournament afforded the Boys Club team an opportunity to participate with area high schools that included Darien, Ludowici, and Louisville. Later a Christmas Holidays Tournament was inaugurated that featured the Boys Club's team and Savannah's Black High schools that were not allowed to participate in the *Savannah Morning News'* Invitational Christmas tournament.

Walter is married to Mary Frank Simmons. They are parents of three adult children, Walter Jr., Ronald and Sandra.

They have eight grandchildren and four great-grand children.

Walter has enjoyed and exceptional career as an educator. He has served Savannah-Chatham County's Public School System as a classroom teacher, a special project teacher, a principal, an executive director, and an Area Assistant Superintendent.

As a classroom teacher, Walter received the Mary Calder Scholarship to study The New Math Concepts at Northwestern University with the idea of introducing those concepts to the teachers of the local system.

He also helped to pioneer integration of the school system by successfully servicing as the first Black to service as the first Black to serve as principal of a formerly all white elementary school.

A lifetime member of St. James A.M.E. Church, Walter has served the Church in various capacities and leadership.

He was been Sunday School teacher, Class leader, trustee, Steward Board Pro-tem, Lay President, Senior Usher, van driver, photographer, delegate to conferences local, district, state and national.

Socially and fraternally, Walter is a former president of Beta Phi Lambda Chapter of Alpha Phi Alpha Fraternity, the Falcons Club, the Mutual Benevolent Society, Beach High School's Class of 1946. He pioneered class reunions in Savannah, served as the first Chair of the reunions.

Currently, he serves as Chaplain of the Frogs Club and advisor to the Frank Callen Boys and Girls Club Alumni Association.

His citations and awards include Alpha Phi Alpha Fraternity Man of the Year, 1946 Class Leadership Award, Savannah Branch Yamacraw Association for outstanding service and contributions to establishing the Negro Heritage Tour Trail, Boys Club of America Keystone Award, Teacher of the Year, Mutual of the Year, Citation-Greater Savannah Athletic Hall of Fame, Enshrinement-Beach High School Athletic Hall of Frame.

*In Praise of Walter Bruce Simmons*
By Lester B. Johnson Jr. Ph.D.

I really do not remember when I first met Walter B. Simmons. He has said that we were together in Mrs. Gertie Thomas' first grade class at East Broad Street School. However, I do remember him from our high school days and our friendship has been one of mutual admiration for each other that has continued to this day. I think the best way that I can describe him is by the introduction speech I made when he was being honored by the Greater Savannah Athletic Hall of Fame. His citation was for his untiring and dedicated work with the Frank Callen Boys (now the Frank Callen Boys' and Girls' Club)

Ladies and Gentlemen, it is a extreme pleasure to perform this task tonight, because the man that I am to present has been a close friend of mine for many years. He is a man whom I've esteemed for his unselfishness to the youth of Savannah. I concur with many of you that these efforts have gone unnoticed until tonight; but tonight we have come to the MOUNTAIN!

My skills and talent lie in the artistic realm rather than the athletic realm, so with your kind permission, I would like to paint a portrait for you; an eastside Black youth – two brothers and many sisters – strong family ties and pride – parents who insisted on scholarship, courtesy, religion and concern for one's fellow beings – Beach High School student – volunteer worker and coach at Frank Callen Boys' – Navy veteran – Baron's Social and Athletic Club – varsity athlete in football and basketball – athletic scholarship to Tuskegee University – Frank's little brother – Fierce competitor, but friendly adversary

## COLOR HIM "FORTY-NINE"

Graduated from Savannah State University – married a basketball star – taught and coached at Walker High School, Moses Jackson School – volunteered for a Pilot Math and Reading Program – Director, Boys' Club – Athletic Director and Coach – all sports; basketball, baseball, softball, table tennis – organized and coached the JETS basketball team – founded and directed the first high school holiday basketball tournament – counselor, mediator, friend, father figure to hundreds – nurtured city's first four sport varsity athlete – watched former athletes earn scholarships to Division I Universities such as Marquette and Indiana – another athlete to play on three different City Christmas Tournament Championship teams – local high schools and colleges clamoring for his boys – impeding delinquency – insisting on discipline and good sportsmanship – respected, admired, idolized and loved.

## COLOR HIM "THE MAN"

Principal at Thirty Eighth Street School, Thirty Seventh Street School, Spencer Elementary School – member of the Board of Directors, Frank Callen Boys' Club – Treasurer, Savannah Football Officials Association – President of the Mutual – Vice President of Alpha Phi Alpha fraternity – Trustee, St. James AME Church – Phi delta Kappa – trusted friend, devoted son, affectionate brother, brother-in-law-, uncle – understanding father – loving and devoted husband – a man's kind of man.

## COLOR HIM "WALTER BRUCE '49' SIMMONS"

# Part Three

**Moments Cheering the Simmons**
**in**

**Education**

**Sports**

**Civic and Social Activities**

**Religion and Church Affairs**

Cheers and Citations

For

Excellence came to the Simmons through the following sources in
Savannah, Ga.:

1) Frank Callen Boys and Girls Club
2) The Beach Institute Preservation Group
3) Tisdell Cottage Foundation
4) Integration of Public Schools
5) History and Future of Beach-Cuyler High Schools
6) The Old Fort Reunion
7) Greek fraternities and Sororities
8) St. James A.M.E. Church
9) Savannah Morning News
10) Savannah Herald
11) Savannah Tribune
12) The Mutual Benevolent Society

# Cheers in Education

There is no esteem in achievements for Black Old Fort Savannahians, none, more prestigious, than achievements recognized for high, higher or highest attainments in education—individually or by groups. The Simons qualify in both categories.

In summary, the outstanding achievements and special recognitions of the Simmons reflected a panoramic point-of-view in citing events from education, sports, civic activities, and cheers from religion.

Certain achievements were selected to reflect depth and breadth of each category and because of the book's limitation, many specific events were left out. For that I implore you and the Simmons to forgive me. The Simmons achieved so much in superlatives than these pages could report.

From 1920 through the years, the Simmons as a family or individuals have been with groups and programs in Savannah, Ga., that struggled to improve and advance education in Savannah, Ga., especially for Black pupils in public schools. During the segregated years, the Simmons with other Savannahians brought better schools, and when Savannah became victorious in desegregating the public schools, the Simmons served in leadership revealing elements of the democratic dream.

Downs cited East Broad Street School Beach Cuyler high schools and Savannah State University as Walter Bruce Simmons' educational segregated background.

Downs wrote "time can thin his hair, slow his stride and bend his back, it can't however diminish the aura of authority and confidence Walter Simmons wears like an old favorite sweater."

Downs wrote that Walter Bruce Simmons at the time of Down's retirement he was 70 years old and 10 years into his retirement. It was Walter Bruce Simmons who became the first Black principal of a formerly all white public school in Savannah, Ga. "I took pride in my job—period." Downs quoted Simmons as saying Walter cited two examples of how he solved problems involving a white pupil with a Black teacher and a Black student with a White teacher. He used the same discipline measure in both situations.

The measure worked. Walter Bruce Simmons began teaching before becoming a principal at 1960's in segregated black school. He started as a teacher at Moses Jackson Elementary School and Cuyler Jr. High School before he served as a principal at the 38th

Street School. Then one day Downs wrote, Simmons got the call! He would become the first Black principal of the all white 37ᵗʰ street public school.

Walter's wife, Mary, said "If anybody could do it, it was Walter Bruce Simmons—with love and firmness."

Walter says "I enjoyed my years at 37ᵗʰ Street School. The Lord placed me there, and I set the tone."

Simons also praised his faculty and staff for their commitment and dedications to make school integration the success that it became it Savannah, Ga. The Simmons, one and all, stand tall in desegregating Savannah's public schools.

<u>Integration changed Savannah's Public School and Savannah as a City</u>

Walter Bruce Simmons, Raleigh Bryant and Dorothy Campbell, three of the first Black Savannahians to be assigned principalships to formerly all white public schools in Savannah Georgia. They shared in agreement all of their accounts and evaluations in relating of the uncertainties, stresses, and conflicts Savannahia faced in integrating Savannah, Ga.'s public schools and Savannah its self.

They tell of the following and more:

1.  White flight
2.  The problems of busing
3.  Fears of saying and doing the wrong things
4.  White teachers were reluntant to visit Black neighborhoods
5.  Lack of classroom space
6.  Schools were not given the needed supplies
7.  Schools were being segregated all over again
8.  But they also spoke of signs for "white only" being removed.


Dorothy Campbell led others into moving into areas recently open to Blacks that would have been for "whites only." Edward and Dorothy Campbell also detailed in their evaluations of desegregation evolving into integration that many Black Savannahians business could no longer depend exclusively on the purchases of Black Savannahians. Many Black business that depended wholly on Black purchases were forced to close.

The Simmons Supported: King-Tinsdell Cottage Foundation located at 500 E. Harris Street, Savannah, GA 31401. Dr. Charles J. Elmore Coordinator of the 2008 Beach Institute Lecture Series, Beach Historic Neighborhood: A Legacy from the Slave Period.

Moderated by: Edna Jackson, City of Savannah, Saturday April 5, 2008 at 5:00 pm at First Congregational Church 421 Habersham Street Savannah, GA 31401. Guest speaker Debbie Allen of *The Amistad Project*: Importance of Telling the Story of Slavery. Moderated by: Dr. Ja Jahannes Sunday April 6, 2008, 3:00 pm, First African Baptist Church 23 Montgomery Street Savannah, GA 31401. The series co-hosted by the Alumni chapter of Delta Sigma Theta sorority. Funding provided by: City of Savannah. Series sponsors: The Savannah Bank and Coldwell Banker Platinum Partners.

Walter Simmons was principal of Thirty-seventh Street Elementary School 310 East 37th Street Savannah, Georgia 31401 received a letter September 9. 1971 from Robert I. Srozier, Member of Board of Public Education and Thord M. Marshall, Ph.D. was Superintendent of Education. Mr. Strozier writes "I would like to thank you for the courageous and humane professionalism you and your staff have shown this first week of school. You are good people. Although I speak essentially for myself, I know the elected and professional School Board members are all very proud of the way you have made this first week a success despite the faces and noises of adversity all around you.

Let me lapse into a little colloquial lingo and say—let's hang in there; we're better than they are. Please call me if I may help you in any way. And thanks again!"

Another letter of recognition came from Brother Prince A. Jackson, Jr., Ph.D. President of Alpha Phi alpha Fraternity, Inc. The letter written March 6, 2002 regarding Presentations of Plaque to Walter Simmons on Sunday March 17, 2002 at St. James A.M.E. Church during its 11:00 am Worship Service.

## Alpha Phi Alpha Fraternity, Inc.
## Beta Phi Lambda Chapter

**To: Brother of Alpha Phi Alpha Fraternity, Inc.**

**From: Brother Prince A. Jackson, Jr. Ph.D., President**

**Re: Presentation of Plaque to Brother Walters B. Simmons on Sunday, March 17, 2002 at St. James A.M.E. Church during its 11:00 A.M. Worship Service**

It was announced and received joyfully at the January 24, 2002 meeting of Beta Phi Lambda Chapter that Brother Walter B. Simmons had been honored in December, 2001 by the Frank Callen Boys and Girls Club with the dedication and naming of the gymnasium for him in recognition of *Ms* unselfish and dedicated work with inner city young people over a period of several decades. This honor bestowed on him was also bestowed upon our great Fraternity by virtue of bis close identification and membership in the Fraternity.

On <u>Sunday, March 17, 2002,</u> Beta Phi Lambda will also bestow high honors on Brother Simmons with the presentation of a special plaque at St. James A.M.E. Church, 632 East Broad Street, during the 11:00 A.M. Worship Service. Brother Simmons is a long time member of St. James and this event will provide his fellow church members with an opportunity to congratulate him and his family.

I am appealing to all Alphas to attend and demonstrate our fraternal love for our brother; I am asking all Alphas to spread the word so that our inactive Brothers will come and increase the number of Brothers in attendance. We will be seated in a section of the Church reserved for us.

St. Paul told us that the Lord loves a cheerful giver and that we cannot give to the Lord more than He will give to us. I am asking each Brother to give Brother Robert Ray at least a $7 donation (7 Jewels) prior to the service so that he can present a check to the Church from us. He will have signed check with Mm and will only have to fill in the amount donated by the Brothers just prior to presenting the check. Be sure to have a few extra dollars to put in the regular collection.

Brother Simmons has been loyal and generous with his time and service to Beta Pi Lambda more than three decades. This is our opportunity to let him and his Church know how much we appreciate him and his contributions to mankind. He is best described by MT 25:31-40.

I look forward to seeing you on March 17, 2002.

# Cheers in Sports

THE BARONS SOCIAL CLUB, INC.
Noble Teens of Reception 1944-1948

At the beginning of the school year—1944-1945, Beach High School was void of an athletic program. Additionally, social activities for students were almost non existent. To fill this void, Walter B. (49) Simmons inspired the inception of a teen age boys club. The Club chose the name Barons and invited Mr. P. W. Cooper to be their advisor. The Barons took it upon themselves to provide the school and the community with a quality athletic program, refined social activities as well as make positive contributions to the community at large.

The Barons were very successful in carrying out their objectives. They became extremely popular and provided many outstanding parties and formal dining and dance affairs under the astute leadership of their advisor, Mr. Cooper and their president, Walter B. (49) Simmons. The Barons became highly respected. Parents felt at ease about having their teens attend the Barons well chaperoned affairs. They also had a team of designated dancers, Bradley Seabrook, Frank Baldwin, Walter Cleveland, Edward Ellis and Walter Simmons, who saw that all of the unescorted girls and wall flowers got to dance.

Athletically, The Barons fielded basketball and football teams. The teams played military teams and local community teams. Mr. Staley was the basketball coach and James "Tishay" Brown coached the football team. The teams were adopted by the students as their own and came to the games and cheered the teams. Most conspicuous were two girls clubs, the Demoiselles and the TAGS, who attended games in cheer leader out fits, including pom-poms.

At the beginning of the 1945-46 school year, the Barons, through Clifford Hardwick, Frank Baldwin, Walter Simmons and Mr. P. Cooper were instrumental in restarting the athletic program at Beach.

*Louis Rivers, Ph.D.*

*1416 Claremont Circle*
*Savannah, Georgia/31415*
*May 5, 2009*

*Dear Sonnie,*

*As usual, since I was enshrined as a citation honoree, in 1976, I was in attendance at the recent Greater Savannah Athletic Hall of Fame Athletic Banquet. Of course, you were at your usual top in showmanship ability in capturing the audience, entertaining and keeping their attention.*

*During the responses by the honorees, one of them stated that "When I was playing, we had only three teams, B.C., Savannah High and commercial High. That statement probably went over your head as well as some of the people in attendance. But to the Bach High Nation, that was a dagger into an old wound! Prior to this person coming onto the athletic fields of Savannah, Georgia. There was Coach Joe Greene and his Beach High Bull Dogs. They were perennial state champions in basketball and Regional Champions in football. Many of his players had gone on to outstanding careers at the collegiate level. In 1939, Beach High participated in basketball tournament of state champions from the segregated states. There were teams from the deep South, Midwest, Texas and Oklahoma, just to name a few names. This team was dubbed the Raggedy Eight from Georgia, by the adoring fans. They finished second-by one point! They were called the "Raggedy Eight", not for their play, but because of their lack of changing uniforms and a warm-up suit! In 1945-1946, Beach High School's state championship team was deemed a "Dream Team" by their legendary Coach, Joe Greene. John Rousakis and Savannah High were also State champions, as you heard during the banquet. The Savannah morning News and the Savannah Evening Press were full of news about the Blue Jackets I challenge you to find articles about the Beach Bull Dogs. Some forward thinking nameless people tried to arrange a secret game between the two teams. No dice! 194-47, found both teams repeating, still no play off game."*

*Charles Perry, a Beach alumnus, played four years at Tuskegee, 1939, 40, 41 & 42, when they were national Black College Champions. He was all American during his Junior and Senior years. Perry, a member of the "Raggedy Eight" also was a super star in basket ball at Tuskegee. He was* all conference four years and All American two years. He also lettered in Tennis and Baseball. Upon Graduating, he was signed by the St. Louis Hawks, becoming the first Savannah athlete to sign a pro-contract.

Your cousin Marcus and I had several confrontations during his tenure with sports writing for the savannah Morning news. He seemed to be very reluctant to give coverage to schools, other than B.C., Savannah High, Jenkins and Groves.

So that honoree, who only knew of B.C., commercial and Savannah High had no way of knowing there were other schools playing in the 1950's. I have no grudge with him. Maybe he thought that our schools were not playing sports! The Morning News almost ignored them completely!

I guess what I'm trying to say is, when I see athletes of the 1930's, 40's and 50's honored and no representatives from Beach, Johnson and Tompkins, fro that era, it bothers me. But when some one says there were no teams, in that era, other than B.C., Commercial and Savannah High that really upsets me!! That whole generation will not be considered for enshrinement. And that's sad, because it is so unfair!

During John Rousakis term as mayor, we got to be real good friends. When I was assigned to integrate his old school 37th Street Elementary he would frequently come by to lend moral support. We often kidded each other about that basketball game that we didn't get to play.

Sonnie, I am venting on you because you have impressed me as being a fair person and I somehow think you really care!

Very respectfully,

Walter B. Simmons
(912) 236-7496

**THE SIMMONS FAMILY**
ATHLETIC LEGACY

**SALUTES THE 2005 HONOREE**

***CAPTAIN FRANK E. SIMMONS***
BASKETBALL-FOOTBALL
CLASS OF 1987 (ORGINAL CLASS)

***WALTER B. (49) SIMMONS***
BASKETBALL-FOOTBALL-SOFTBALL-SWIMMING
CLASS OF 1988

***EUGENIA SIMMONS GLOVER***
BASKETBALL
CLASS OF 1990

***JUANITA SIMMONS MARKS****
BASKETBALL
CLASS OF 1993

# FRANK CALLEN BOYS & GIRLS CLUB ALUMNI AND FRIENDS ASSOCATIONS

Date:   January 13, 2011

To:   All Alumni and Friends

From:   Raymond Rouse, President
        Frank Callen Boys & Girls Club Alumni & Friends Association

Re:   FY 2011 Honoree Banquet and Membership Drive

As we embarked upon another year, it is time for us to honor the people and organizations that aided in the sustaining and life-span of the Frank Callen Boys and Girls Club. Our nominating committee has met; the decisions have been made. The 2011 Honorees are as follows:

1. St. John Baptist Church
2. Ms. Sarah Mills Hodge
3. Mr. Raymond Rouse
4. Mr. John Delaware

Please come join us as we honor the people and organizations that have offered their support over the years. Let's make this a momentous occasion. Your support is needed for such a worthy event. At this time, the Association is also reaching out to encourage former Boys Clubbers and Friends to come join and/or renew their membership.

We are asking that a contribution of $50.00 be submitted which covers the cost of the banquet and the FY 2011 membership. If you have a guest that would like to attend the Honoree's Banquet, the cost will be $30.00 per person. The banquet will be held in the Eden Room at the Temple of Giory Community Church. The doors will open at 5:00 p.m. which will allow us time to meet and greet all our members and friends. The program will begin promptly at 6:00 p.m.

It would be a tremendous blessing to the Honoree's and the Association if you would grace us with your presence. A program has been planned with you and your family in mind. Looking forward to seeing you there!

Yours in Youth

*Raymond Rouse*

Dear Loyal Member:

On behalf of Raymond Rouse, President and fellow members of the Frank Callen Boys and Girls Club Alumni and Friends Association, I take this opportunity to express our sincere appreciation for your contribution of membership and attendance at our annual award dinner. We are deeply grateful for your support and generosity.

It is through the support of individuals like yourself that we are able to continue to strengthen our programs, and to develop new and innovative projects to help serve the members of the Frank Callen Boys and Girls Club.

Again, thank you for making our mission a reality. Sincerely,

*Floyd*

Floyd Adams, Jr.
Membership Chair

# Cheers For Civic And Social Activities

APPRECIATION DAY FOR WALTER B. (49) SIMMONS

Frank Callen Boys and Girls Club

July 5, 1969

The Frank Callen Boys Club and varsity alumni Jets celebrated an Appreciation Day for Walter B. Simmons, who recently retried as coach and athletic director at the club. While supposedly on his way to a dinner date, "49" was prevailed upon to stop by the Club. Upon entering he found, to his surprise, the club gaily decorated, a large audience made up almost entirely of boys and girls he had coached or worked with during his 21 years of a volunteer worker and coach, and a professional band, Clay White's Organ Combo, entertaining. John Maker, brilliant as master of ceremonies, gave the occasion, Nat Hamilton read a scripture lesson, and Edgar Lee Maxwell played "49's" favorite song magnificently on his organ. Recognition of the honored guest and his family was done by Eugene Johnson. Mrs. Alice Simmons, "49's" mother was complimented for her son, and presented a corsage. Mrs. "49" was presented an orchid, a basket of red roses and a beautiful plaque inscribed "TO THE MOST UNDERSTANDING COACH'S WIFE IN APPRECIATION OF SHARING YOUR HUSBAND WITH US IT HAS BEEN AND WILL ALWAYS BE A PRICELESS TREASURE" For many years Mrs. 49 served a official scorekeeper, chauffeur chaperon and concessioner for the Boys Club. Little Sandra Simmons was presented a rose and Manker promised to let little 49 win that basketball game he has always wanted to win from him. Joe Murray Rivers gave the history of The Man as 49 was referred to throughout the program. He told how the Man started the athletic program from scratch.

How he coached two baseball teams and a softball team simultaneously during the summer, and worked with two basketball teams during the winter, and worked with ping-pong and other games between seasons. He told of the pride instilled in these teams and of the many exciting "first time" trips made over the years. He told of the several cars, many sets of tires and gallons of gasoline used up and the many sets of athletic uniforms The Man had to sponsor. How—over the years he became counselor, friend, brother, father as well as coach earned the confidence, respect and admiration of the entire community. Murray closed by saying how the Man had stimulated them to work together to earn money to purchase their first set of uniforms and how much it meant to the players to be the first uniformed sand otters. This created a sense of pride that exists to this day. An impressive plaque was presented to 49 for each sport that he introduced and coached at the club. The Ping pong plaque was presented by Peter Ward, who helped to build the first ping pong table at the club, and Marion Holmes, both members of teams that won ping pong championships in regional tournaments in Wilmington and Durham, N.C. Petro Greene, the city's first four sport varsity man, and Lawrence Hutchins, currently bandmaster at Liberty High School, presented the baseball plaque. As a prelude to the awarding of the basketball plaque, Manker cited Ed Daniels, B.J. Gadsden and an impressive list of outstanding basketball player who got their start at the Boys Club. Al Walls, Rocky Heyward, James Holmes, Ed Days, Jimmy Burke and Frank Brown presented a magnificent basketball plaque bearing the engraved names of 60 former Boys Club and Jets basketball players.

They were inscribed TO THE MOST DEVOTED LOYAL UNDERSTANDING AND SKILLFUL COACH Miss Wilma Grant presented a gift certificate on behalf of the LaBelles, a girls softball and basketball team formed at the club. Many people made outstanding contributions to the club through 49. Among those signaled out for acknowledgment were, Ed Campbell, John Grant, John miles, Edgar" Joe Louis" Moore, Russell Ellington, Leonard D. Law, Thomas Milledge, Frank Simmons, Richard Washington, Robert Washington, and Ted Wright, Sr. Also, William J. "Sloppy Joe" Bellinger, William Harris and Maurice Smith. Deceased.

## The Frank Callen Boys & Girls Club

This year has been an amazing year at the Frank Callen Boys & Girls Club. Here at the Boys & Girls Club, the youth are afforded numerous opportunities and are exposed to new and rewarding experiences. The Boys & Girls Club has a number of groups, programs, and activities to offer youth of all ages. Just last month one of the teen leadership groups, known as the Keystone Club, was afforded the opportunity to travel to the National Keystone Leadership Conference held in Orlando, Fla. Through this trip the teens were able to attend leadership sessions, meet teens from all over the world, trade project ideas, meet famous actors, singers, and public officials as well as engage in new/fun leisure activities. Trips like these are opportunities most young people seldom have the opportunity to experience, but here at the Boys & Girls Club exposing youth to new and positive experiences is what we're all about. Through the Boys and Girls we also do events geared towards the community as a whole as well as our showing appreciation to the parents. By having events like, "Parent Appreciation", the Boys & Girls Club is able to give back to those who have participated and supported us in some way, shape, or form throughout the year. At the Boys & Girls Club we also recognize that without the support and generosity of others we would not be able to do some of the things that we do. Organizations like the Boys & Girls Alumni Association are intricate part in helping to sponsor events, trips, and programs as well as giving back to and spending quality time with the youth of the Boys & Girls Club. The Boys Girls Club works overtime to help mold and nurture the youth into becoming responsible and productive young adults. This past year the Club teamed up with Savannah State University to help expose the older youth to different college experiences.

The teens attended the Roland Martin and Spike Lee motivational speaking forums at Savannah State University as well as participated in college torus to get better acquainted with the University and the pros of receiving a post-secondary education. The Boys & Girls Club also takes pride in our youth that ago above and beyond. Here at the Boys & Girls Club we honor those who do exceptionally well in all areas by nominating them as Youth of the Year. This month our Youth of the Year, Jared Kolleh, competed in the Youth of the Year Conference in Atlanta, Ga. This conference was very fun and exciting and allowed the youth to mix and mingle as well as compete in friendly oratorical competition. Overall the

Boys & Girls Club is a not only a Positive Place for Kids, but also a place where they can learn and grow. If you are looking for an exciting place for children to learn and grown or would like to volunteer, the Boys & Girls Club has something for you.

## FRANK CALLEN BOYS AND GIRLS CLUB ALUMNI
## MAKES PRESENTATIONS

The Frank Callen Boys & Girls Club Alumni and Friends Association, Inc. presented the Boys and Girls Club of the Coastal Empire Athletic Department and the Keystone Club leadership and service program with donations to augment their programs.

The presentation was made Tuesday, March 15th by the new 2011 President Raymond Rouse and other members and friends of the Frank Callen Boys and Girls Club Alumni and Friends Association, Inc.

## FRANK CALLEN BOYS & GIRLS ALUMNI ASSOCATION
## ELECTS NEW OFFICERS

The Frank Callen Boys and Girls Club Alumni Association has elected Officers for the 2011 and 2012 term. Officers are: President Mr. Raymond Rouse, Vice President-Karen Datts, Secretary-Ms. Vergie Williams, and Assistant Secretary—Ms. Dorothy Scott, Treasurer—Mr. James Stewart, Financial Secretary—Mr. Joseph Rivers, Chaplin—Mr. Charlie Brown, Parliamentarian—Mr. Floyd Adams, Jr., and Advisor—Mr. Walter Simmons.

OUTGOING PRESIDENT'S MESSAGE
Walter B. Simmons

The State of the Society
December 12, 1977

Fellow Mutuals and Beautiful Ladies—

Greetings:

Members, committee chairmen and officers, thank you for your support, cooperation, and courtesies extended to me during my term as president. I have appreciated you totally and your willingness to go an extra mile with me. Ladies, I am especially grateful to you for your understanding, patience and graciousness in sharing your husbands with me these three (3) years.

As your president, I have tried to lead you, serve you and represent you. Some things I have done well, and others not so well. I am sure I messed up some things too. But in all things I have given my best for the Mutuals.

I have appreciated the honor, the prestige and the trust of being your president, especially at this historic time.

Thus far in my life time, I have been fortunate to have received some recognitions and awards. But when I look back and reflect over my life time, I will think of this organization, its great history, proud traditions and the great men, past and present—who served it as president. For me to be listed among these men—will ever be among the high lights of my life.

I leave the presidency now with mixed emotion. There are several plans that have not yet reached fruition. There are several problems that have not been resolved. But we are still together we have taken some new directions— while maintaining traditions that are dear to us. This progress! The Society is together! The Society is well! The Society is moving!

Among the notable accomplishments during my administration were: (1) our participation in the observance of the 100th Emancipation Program (Mutuals played prominent roles in our community) (2) the beginning of 1976 and 1977 with prayer breakfasts that included the presence of our wives, (3) the adoption of our Constitution and By-Laws, (4) a system of rotation the hosting of meetings, (5) establishing a savings account to be used for investments, (6) most important to me, a feeling of fellowship and good will among all Mutuals, and (7) including the wives and sweethearts in a Christmas Dinner Meeting to close out the year and my administration.

However, I leave the presidency with no regrets and no apprehensions, because of the outstanding team of officers that will assure its leadership.

Having sserved the past three years as president and not missing a single meeting—I am more than ready to pass on this Gavel of Trust, Leadership, responsibility and prestige to Willie Fleming and the other new officers. I wish them God Speed and Good Luck and pledge my support and co-operation!

To you my fellow Mutals, I offer this challenge—that you re-dedicate yourselves to the ideals, traditions and concepts of Mutuals, and that you pledge to attend more meetings and participate in more Mutual functions.

Remember, we are like grains of sugar in a cup of coffee. The more-more of us "stir" in fellowship with each other, the sweeter will be our cup of coffee. Sometimes it becomes a sacrifice to stir, but it might just be your grain that makes the difference.

# Cheers from the Church and Religion

In cheering the Simmons in religion, the cheers began in 1920, when the Simmons first came to Savannah, and the cheers continued to this present moment the Simmons will always be remembered & cherished, as outstanding members of St. James A.M.E. church.

## COMMERATING THE SIMMONS FAMILY LEGACY
## AT ST. JAMES A.M.E. CHURCH
1920-2012

Walter Wally Simmons*
Mens' Bible Class Teacher
1884-1935

Marie Simmons Kennedy*
Missionary Society, President
Stewardess Bd. No.1, Senior Choir,
Volunteer Musician, Lay Organization

Nellie Simmons Oxner*
Sunday School Teacher
Organist—Senior Choir

Captain Frank E, Simmons*
Steward, Adult Bible Class,
President—Rev. A.B. Wilson
Male Chorus, Soloist
1921-1990

Eugenia Simmons D. Glover*

D. Alice Simmons*
Missionary Society, President,
Stewardess Bd. No.1, Gospel Chorus
Lay Organization
1893-1970

John A. Simmons*
Chorister and Soloist—Sr. Choir
Bible Class
1914-1944

Bessie Simmons Hannah
Stewart, President—Missionary Society,
President Stewardess Bd. No. 1, Sunday
School Teacher, Vacation Bible School
Teacher, Hospitality Committee, Lay
Organization

Alma Simmons Campbell*
Sunday School, Junior Choir, Young
Women's Progressive Club
1921-1960

Steward, Missionary, Stewardess, Sunday School Teacher, Vacation Bible School Teacher, Hospitality Committee, Senior Choir, Young Women's Progressive Club, Lay Organization, Missionary Society School and Choirs, Young Women's 1923-2008

Walter B. Simmons, Jr.
Trustee, President—A.B. Wilson Male Chorus, B.S. Hannah Chorus, Sunday School, Boy Scouts

Mary Frank Simmons*
President-Senior Choir, President Missionary Society, Stewardess Bd. No. 1, Vacation Bible School Teacher, Hospitality Club, Lay Organization, Pastor's Aid Board

Juanita Simmons Marks*
Sunday School Teacher, Vacation Bible School Teacher, Junior Choir, Senior Choir, Voluntary Musician for Sunday School and Choirs, Young Women's

Progressive Club (1928-1988)

Sandra Simmons Fuller
Gussie White Choir, Missionary Society Sunday School

Walter B. Simmons, Sr.
Pro-tem Steward Board, President, Lay Organization, Trustee, Sunday School Audiovisual Specialist, First church volunteer van diver

From 1920 until 2012, the Sun has shone on the Simmons family in Savannah, Ga. From Marie Simmons through Juanita Simmons, the Simmons family individually and collectively made outstanding contribution through the continuation of the black Culture. They are hailed for their achievements in education, sports, public affairs, and religion.

There is no question as to what the Simmons family has done. Questions however are asked. Who and what Simmons will step into past shoes to carry on what the Simmons have started and left for the next generations of Simmons, follow.

Presently 2012, the Simmon's are leaving; Ten grandchildren, twenty-two great grandchildren, and ten great great grandchildren.

Marie Simmons had no children.

John Simmons married Estella Doby. They had no children.

Nellie Simmons had no children.

Ephriam Alston married to Lucille Singleton. They had three children: Dr. Charles Alston, Anne Alston, and Kay Alston

Bessie Simmons Hannah married to Bingley Hannah. They had two sons: Bingley S. Hannah, Jr. and Frank Hannah.

Alma Simmons Campbell married to Edward Campbell had two children. The first child, a girl, died in infancy. The second, also a girl was named for Eugenia Simmons, "Jeanie"

Eugenia Jeanie Simmons Durden—Glover She had two children with John Durden, John G. Durden Jr., and Patricia Durden.

Walter Bruce Simmons married to Mary Fran had two biological sons one legally adopted daughter. They are: Walter B. Simmons, Jr. Ronald J. Simmons, and Sandra Marie Simmons.

Juanita Simmons she was married to Earl Dexter. They had three children—Dr. Earl Dexter Marks, Jr. Phillip Marks, Regina Alice Marks

# Appendix A

## The Simmons Family Reuion
## and
## The Simmons Family Tree

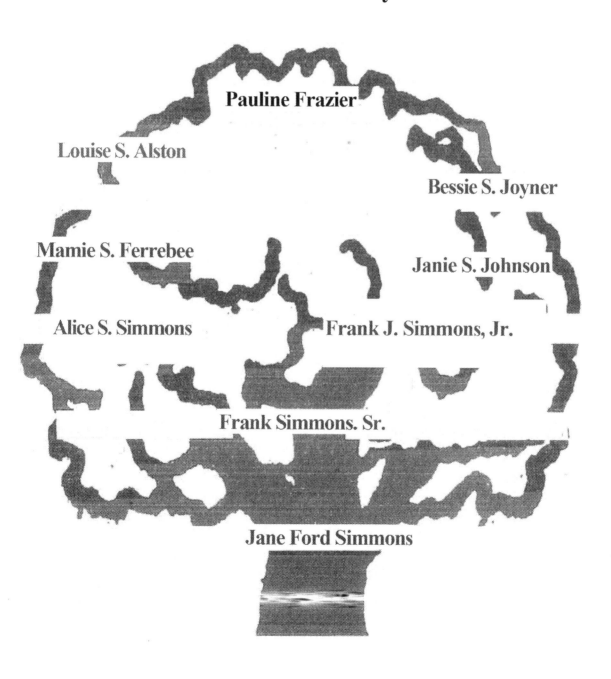

Pauline Frazier

Louise S. Alston

Bessie S. Joyner

Mamie S. Ferrebee

Janie S. Johnson

Alice S. Simmons

Frank J. Simmons, Jr.

Frank Simmons. Sr.

Jane Ford Simmons

The family reunions were annual programs planned and sponsored by The Simmons. The reunions began in the 1930's and have been repeated annually over the years. They consisted largely of evaluating and rewarding members of the Simmons family for outstanding achievements in individually and collectively. Many of the reunions were held at St. James A.M.E. church in Savannah, Ga.

This is the Simmons Family Tree of Frank Simmons, Sr. & Jane Ford Simmons. (It was taken from a family reunion program):

1) Pauline Frazier        2) Bessie S. Joyner

3) Louise S. Alston        4) Mamie S. Ferrebee

5) Janie S. Johnson        6) Alice S. Simmons

7) Frank J. Simmons, Jr.

(and of course Daisy Alice Simmons & Walter Wallie Simmons and their family)

Walter "Wally" Simmons

March 19, 1883-January 23, 1935

Daisy Alice Simmons

May 12, 1893-July 1972

Marie Simmons Fabian Kennedy

March 4, 1910-

John Augustus Simmons

June 1914-

Nellie Simmons Williams Oxner

August 23, 1916-

Bessie Simmons Hannah

November 12, 1919-

Frank Edward Simmons

July 26, 1921-


Eugenia Simmons Durden Glover

August 14, 1923-


Walter Bruce Simmons

October 29, 1926-


Juanita Simmons Marks

August 17, 1927-August 14, 1988


Walter "Wally Simmons and Daisy Alice Simmons were married on March 8, 1908 at Campbell Chapel AME Church in Bluffton, S.C. Walter was buried in Mullins Hole Cemetery, near Okatie, S.C., his birthplace. Daisy Alice Simmons was buried in Magnolia Gardens in Savannah, Ga. John A. Simmons, is buried in Lincoln Memorial Cemetery. Marie, Frank and Juanita are also buried in Magnolia Gardens.


## The Simmons Family Reunion


The family reunions were annual programs planned and sponsored by The Simmons. The reunions began in the 1930's and have been repeated annually over the years. They consisted largely of evaluating and rewarding members of the Simmons family of outstanding achievements in individually and collectively. Many of the reunions were held at St. James A.M.E. church in Savannah, Ga.

**The Simmons Family Reunion**

**Friday evening, July 9, 1993**

**7:00 p.m.**

**Carey Hilliard's Restaurant**

**11111 Abercorn Street**
**Savannah, Georgia**

## FRANK AND JANE FORD SIMMONS FAMILY HISTORY

Families are like a tree. If the roots and limbs are well cared for, loved and pruned, it will not die. The seeds will survive, go forth and become strong in greatness and prosperity.

Many years ago **Jane Ford** was born in **Charleston, SC. At an early age she migrated to Bluffton, SC** and joined Campbell A.M.E. Church.

**She met Frank Simmons** and was united in holy matrimony. This union was blessed with **6 girls and 2 boys**. The stability of this family was grounded on Christian principles. Their economic security was based upon their occupations. Frank was **a farmer** and Jane was a **midwife.**

The family tree was extended as the children united in holy matrimony and bore children. **James and Pauline** were the only offsprings of **Frank and Jane** who did not bear children. The family record shows that **James was three years old** when he died in Bluffton. **Pauline died** in Bluffton at the age of twenty-one.

Frank Simmons, the patriarch of the family, died in Bluffton in 1896. Jane Ford Simmons, matriarch of the family, died in Bluffton in 1922.

The children and grandchildren of Frank and Jane are the branches of the Simmons-Ford Family Tree. These children, because of the limited social, economic, and educational opportunities available to them in Bluffton, SC at the beginnings of the twentieth century, migrated to Savannah, GA and the cities of the North.

**Louise Simmons Alston** was born October 20, 1882. She was joined in holy matrimony to Richard Alston in 1898. They migrated to Savannah in 1917. Eight children were born to this union; three girls and five boys. The mother, Louise, died October 20, 1920 in Savannah. The father, Richard, died November 8, 1926 in Savannah.

The names of the deceased Alston children are: Frank Alston, died in 1917 in Savannah; Clifford, died in 1968 in Cincinnati, OH; Paul Alston, died in 1968 in New York City; Janie Stobert, died in 1974 in New York City; Cornelia A. Pierce, died in Philadelphia, PA, and a baby girl died a few months old. There are two of the original Alstons still living; Edward Alston (deceased) lived in Plainfield, NJ and Ephraim Alston, living in Savannah.

**Bessie Simmons Joiner** was born January 17, 1884. She was joined in holy matrimony to Bertrum Joiner, Sr., in 1901. She was the only child who remained in Bluffton. To this union eleven children were born-six boys and five girls. The father, Bertrum Sr., died February 14, 1961 in Bluffton. The mother, Bessie, died December 15, 1965 in Bluffton.

The names of the deceased children are Flora J. Heyward, who died February 12, 1970 in Bluffton, Archie Fowler who died June 29, 1981 in Washington, DC, Arthur Joiner who died April 27, 1983 in Savannah, Bertrum Joiner, Jr. who died January 28, 1984 in Savannah and James Joiner who died May 11, 1992 in Bluffton, SC. The names of the six living children are Joseph Joiner, Pauline Metcalf and Mary J. Williams of bluffton, Janie J. Jackson of Alexandria, VA, Benjamin Joiner of Hamden, CT and Dorothy J. Singleton of Hilton Head, SC.

**Mamie Simmons Ferrebee** was born September 15, 1886. She was joined in holy matrimony to William Ferrebee December 10, 1906. To this union thirteen children were born-eleven girls and two boys. Three children died at birth. The father, William, died March 26, 1968 in Savannah. The mother, Mamie, died May 14, 1983 in Savannah.

The names of the deceased children are Thomas Ferrebee who died December 23, 1966 in Savannah, Geneva F. Green who died in 1971, Lillian F. Elliott who died July 30, 1971 in Savannah, Louise F. Bowman who died April 5, 1974, Alice F. Hines who died in November 1974 in Savannah. There are five living children. Their names are Henrietta F. Goldwire, Willie Ferrebee and Helen F. Green of Savannah, Mary F. Guest of Brunswick, GA, and Betty F. Green of Bronx, NY.

**Janie Simmons Johnson** was born January 12, 1891. She migrated to Savannah in 1908 where she met Amos Johnson and was united in holy matrimony on October 21, 1909. To this union ten children were born-seven girls and three boys. The father, Amos, died January 13, 1939 in Savannah. The mother, Janie, died December 25, 1963 in Savannah.

The names of the deceased children are Corrie J. Drayton who died September 21, 1942 in Savannah, Elease J. Lamore who died December 12, 1942 in New York City and Otis S. Johnson, Sr. who died on October 30, 1943 in New York City. There are seven living children. Their names are: Paul A. Johnson Bernice J. White and Flora J. Haynes of New York City, Janie Lee Davis of Pritchardville, SC, Annette Johnson, Stanley Johnson and Stella J. Barnes of Savannah.

**D. Alice Simmons** was born May 12, 1893. She was joined in holy matrimony to Walter Simmons on March 1908. To this union eight children were born. Because of her husband's employment as a 1ˢᵗ Class Pilot of the Island Girl, they moved to Savannah, GA in 1920. They became affiliated with St. James A.M.E. Church. Walter (Wallie) Simmons expired January 23, 1925. Alice Simmons served faithfully for over 60 years as a classleader, member of Gospel choir, Christian Women's Association and president of the Stewardess Board No.1. She expired July 16, 1972. Three children are deceased, namely: John A. Simmons who was killed in World War II, November 9, 1944 at St. Marie Dumont, France; Juanita S. Marks passed August 14, 1988 and Frank E. Simmons passed April 27, 1990, both of Savannah, GA.

Her surviving children are Marie S. Kennedy of Savannah, GA, Nellie S. Oxner of Charlotte, NC, Bessie S. Hannah, Eugenia S. Glover and Walter B. Simmons of Savannah, GA and 10 grandchildren, 22 great-grandchildren and 10 great-great grands.

**Frank Simmons** was born February 5, 1895. He migrated to Savannah in 1919. He was joined in holy matrimony to Ida Wright in 1920. The father, Frank, died in August 1977 in Philadelphia. To this union two children were born. A son, Frank, Jr. died when he was an infant. A daughter, Alma s. Campbell, died February 24, 1960 in Savannah.

Mamie Ferrebee was the last survivor of the eight children of Frank and Jane Ford Simmons. As the history closes on the contributions of Frank and Jane Ford Simmons, a new chapter will open as their descendants continue in great numbers. The ideals and goals our ancestors strived for are reflected in the accomplishments of their descendants.

Among us are musicians, laboratory technologists, mechanics, military career personnel, carpenters, teachers, church officials, doctors, I.B.M. Operators, film editors, educational administrators, telephone installers and repairmen, postal service employees, college professors with earned doctorate degrees, retired railroad personnel, retired school teachers and principals, secretaries, owners of businesses, librarians, sales persons, painters, nurses, employment supervisors, hospital administrators, electronic engineers, housewives, former city councilmen, and a member of the North Carolina Literacy Council Board of directors.

The Family History Researched by Estella Johnson Barnes

Revised by

Otis S. Johnson

July 1993

## Programme

Toastmistress. . . . . . . . . . . . . . . . . . . . . . Mrs. Audrey B. Singleton

Prelude. . . . . . . . . . . . . . . . . . . . . . . . . . Mrs. Berneida W. Green

The Opening Selection. . . . . . . . . . . .What A Fellowship" . . . . . Audience

The Occasion and Welcome . . . . . . . . . . . . . . . . . Mrs. Delores L. Laury

The Inspirational Readings . . . . . . . . . . . . . . . . Mrs. Patricia D. Johnson

The Invocation and Blessing. . . . . . . . . . . Mrs. Mary J. Williams, Chaplain

### Dinner

The Duet . . . . . . . . . . . . . . . . . . . Mrs. Adrina Taylor and Mrs. Thelma

The Speaker . . . . . . . . . . . . . . . . . . . . . . . . . .Dr. Otis S. Johnson

The Medley of Tunes . . . . . . . . . . . . . . . . . . . Mrs. Berneida W. Green

Reading of Family History. . . . Mrs. Mary F. Simmons & Mr. Walter B. Simmons

The Memorial Tribute . . . . . . . . . . . . . . . . . Mr. Walter B. Simmons, Sr.

(Mr. James Joiner and Mr. William Metcalf)

The Roll Call and Presentation to Our Senior Cherished Members

by Mrs. Dorothy J. Singleton, Pres. Of the Simmons Family Reunion Association

Honorees: Mrs. Janie Lee J. Davis, Mrs. Henrietta F. Goldwire and Mrs. Pauline J. Metcalf

The Benediction

The Closing Selection        "Blest Be The Tie That Binds" . . . . . Audience

### The Worship Service

St. James A.M.E. Church

Sunday, July 11, 1993—11:00 a.m.

**The Programme Committee**

Mrs. Delories Laury

Mrs. Mary F. Simmons

Mrs. Eugenia S. Glover

**Officers for 1991-1993**

Chairpersons . . . . . . . . . .Mrs. Dorothy J. Singleton & Mrs. Elizabeth Johnson

Historian . . . . . . . . . . . . . . . . . . . . . . . . . . . . .Dr. Otis S. Johnson

Secretary . . . . . . . . . . . . . . . . . . . . . . . . . Mr. Walter B. Simmons, Sr.

Assistant Secretary . . . . . . . . . . . . . . . . . . . . . Mrs. Eugenia S. Glover

Financial Secretary . . . . . . . . . . . . . . . . . . . . .Mrs. Antoinette J. Johnson

Treasurer . . . . . . . . . . . . . . . . . . . . . . . . . . Mrs. Pauline J. Metcalf

Chaplain . . . . . . . . . . . . . . . . . . . . . . . . . . .Mrs. Mary J. Williams

Banquet . . . . . . . . . . . . . . . . . . . . . . . . . . . Mrs. Estella Barnes

Sunshine Committee . . . . . . . Mrs. Delores J. Laury & Mrs. Mary F. Simmons

Travel Consultants . . . . . . . Mrs. Antoinette J. Johnson & Mrs. Delores J. Laury

Family Picnic . . . . .Mr. Ephriam Alston, Mr. Stanley Johnson, Mr. B.S. Hannah, Mr. Diogenese Singleton, Mr. Elmer Barnes and Mr. Walter B. Simmons, Sr.

*THE SIMMONS FAMILY REUNION ASSOCIATION*

Descendants of

*JANE FORD SIMMONS\**
*(1859-1921)*
*&*
*FRANK SIMMONS\**
*(1857-1910)*

"They served Campbell Chapel with great distinction and devotion"

We congratulate you on this auspicious occasion!

**Immediate Descendants**

Louise Simmons Alston\* (1882-1920)

Bessie Simmons Joiner\* (1884-1965)

***Mamie Simmons Ferrebee\* (1886-1983)***

***Pauline Simmons Frazier\* (1888-1909)***

***Janie Simmons Johnson\* (1891-1963)***

***Alice Simmons\* (1893-1972)***

***Frank Simmons\* (1895-1977)***

***\*Deceased***

*Delores Johnson Laury, President*

# Appendix B

Excerpts taken from Campbell Chapel
African Methodist Episcopal Church
Dedicatory Celebration
By
The Right Reverend Henry A. Belin, Jr.
Presiding Bishop Rev. George Welch Brown, Sr.
Presiding Elder Rev. Isaac W. Wilborn, Jr.
Pastor Rev. Benjamin Mitchell, Sr. Local Minster

# Campbell Chapel

## African Methodist Episcopal Church

### Dedicatory Celebration

*"Unless the Lord builds the house, those who build it labor in vain…"*
*Psalm 127:1*

May 23, 2004~4:00 p.m.

**The Right Reverend Henry A. Belin, Jr., Presiding Bishop**
**Reverend George Welch Brown, Sr., Presiding Elder**
**Reverend Isaac W. Wilborn, Jr., Pastor**
**Reverend Benjamin Mitchell, Sr., Local Minister**

# Our Founders

Bishop Richard Allen

Sarah Bass Allen

Richard Allen, the founder and first Bishop of the African Methodist Episcopal Church, was born a slave on February 14, 1760 on the Benjamin Chew estate. Deeply religious from an early, age, Allen was converted at the age of 17. He began preaching in 1780 and was ordained in 1799. Through thrift and industry, he and his brother worked at night to pay for their freedom.

Bishop Allen was married to Sarah Bass Allen (2nd wife), who founded the Women's Missionary Society.

God Our Father

Christ Our Redeemer

Man Our Brother

## Church Officers

| Pastor | Rev. Isaac W. Wilborn, Jr. |
|---|---|
| Local Minister | Rev. Ben Mitchell, Sr. |
| Steward Pro-Tem | Lee Smalls |
| Trustee Pro-Tem | Fred Hamilton |
| Stewardess Board I | Mary Lawyer |
| Stewardess Board II | Mattie Williams |
| Secretary | Peggy Jaynes |
| Financial Secretary | Joan Simmons |
| New Construction Financial Secretary | James Gilliard |
| Building Fund Chairperson | Frank Gadson |
| Sexton | Sharon Brown |
| Yard Staff Chairperson | Isaac Bryant |
| Estelle Johnson WMS President | Vanessa Tiburcio |
| Young People Department Director | Doris Gregory |
| Sons of Allen President | James Gilliard |
| DMC Commissioner | Sharon Brown |
| Musician | Alyce English |
| Christian Education Director | Lucille Kannick |
| Church School Superintendent | Lincoln Kannick |
| Assistant Superintendent | Jacob Martin |
| Primary Class Teacher | Delores Anderson |
| Youth Class Teacher | Romona Wilborn |
| Intermediate Class Teacher | Nellie White |
| Senior Class Teacher | Lee Smalls |
| Adult Class Teacher | Jacob Martin |

### *Weekly Worship Schedule*

| Church School | (Every Sunday) | 9:45 a.m. |
|---|---|---|
| Worship Service | (1st – 4th Sundays) | 11:00 a.m. |
| WMS Worship Service | (5th Sundays) | 11:00 a.m. |
| Prayer Service/Bible Study | (Tuesdays) | 7:00 p.m. |

# MOTHER BETHEL
## AFRICAN METHODIST EPISCOPAL CHURCH

*The oldest parcel of land continuously owned by African Americans
Purchased by Richard Allen in 1791*

419 Richard Allen Avenue
Philadelphia, Pennsylvania 19147
(215) 925-0616 ~ (215) 925-1402-Fax ~ Email: MotherBethel@aol.com

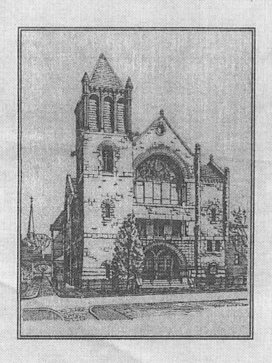

*God our Father*　　　　　*Christ Our Redeemer*　　　　　*Man our Brother*

*The Reverend Dr. Jeffrey N. Leath, Pastor
The Reverend Dr. Winton M. Hill, III, Presiding Elder
The Right Reverend Richard F. Norris, Presiding Bishop*

Richard Allen

Sarah Allen

**THE SECOND BUILDING**
**1805 - 1841**

**FOURTH BUILDING**
**ERECTED 1889 - 1890**
**RESTORED 1987**

**THE THIRD BUILDING**
**1841 - 1898**

# A WORD ABOUT MOTHER BETHEL CHURCH

Mother Bethel Church stands on the oldest piece of land (Sixth Street - near Lombard) continuously owned by African Americans in the United States. Purchased in 1791, this property has been the site of four buildings erected by the congregation for worship and service.

Mother Bethel traces it roots to the Free African Society which was founded in 1787. Originally, the Free African Society was a typical mutual aid society. The members made regular contributions to the treasury, and the funds were used to help members in times of illness or other personal calamity.

When insulted by the trustees of St. George's Methodist Episcopal Church during Morning Prayer, it was a natural transition for the protesting black Methodists to exit the sanctuary, and rally within the structure of their Free African Society. Though not organized to be a church, the Free African Society functioned as a nucleus for a community of believers. Difference over denominational styles and affiliation led to Richard Allen's departure from the Free African Society. By 1791, Allen had signed a contract for this very site to be used by the Society for the erection of a house of worship. This group purchased another plot, and, led by Absalom Jones, became known as the African Episcopal Church of St. Thomas. Absalom Jones became the first African American Episcopal priest in 1804.

Richard Allen, a former slave and Methodist lay preacher, was committed to the Methodist doctrine as the most acceptable way of delivering the gospel to people of color. There is little doubt that Allen continued to nurture those who followed after the 1787 "walk-out." By July 1794 (the same year of the completion of St. Thomas' edifice), Allen was dedicating a building for worship called **Bethel**. A blacksmith shop (purchased in 1793) was dragged by Allen's team of horses to the plot on Sixth Street. The structure was renovated, and the first church was in operation. It has been said that the blacksmith's anvil, became the first pulpit. This makes the symbol dear to African Methodists.

Allen was ordained in 1799 by Francis Asbury, a bishop in the Methodist Episcopal Church. In 1816, Richard Allen called together black Methodists from as far away as Baltimore to create a new Methodist conference. This was the birth of the **African Methodist Episcopal Church. Bishop Richard Allen** was consecrated the first bishop to serve the church. Allen was a champion of the anti-slavery cause, and he became a spokesman for his people on both local and national issues. Cited by David Walker in his *Appeal* as a great leader of his time, Allen was known near and far for courage and zeal.

Bethel Church hosted the first national convention of African Americans (1830). It was a forum for many of the nation's great orators and a stop along the "underground railroad."

The present building was erected in 1889. Visitors will note the beauty and symbolism of the stained glass windows. The building underwent a major renovation in 1987. The pews are original. As a tribute to Richard Allen, Sixth Street (between Pine Street & Lombard Street) was renamed Richard Allen Avenue. Richard Allen, Sarah Allen (his wife), and Morris Brown (the second consecrated bishop of the A.M.E. Church) are entombed on the lower level. Mother Bethel is a worshiping, serving congregation which welcomes visitors to share the legacy and the praise of the God of Bethel.

# RICHARD ALLEN MUSEUM EXHIBIT HALL

**Richard Allen's Pulpit**

**Pews from Blacksmith Shop**

*HISTORY OF*

**CAMPBELL CHAPEL**

**AFRICAN METHODIST EPISCOPAL CHURCH**

Bluffton, South Carolina

The building in which Campbell Chapel A.M.E. Church worships was constructed in 1853 as the Bluffton Methodist Episcopal Church. It was later sold and purchased in 1874 by nine former slaves who were looking for a building in which to establish a church under the auspices of a black denomination spreading over the south call the African Methodist Episcopal Church.

The nine men were Jacob Chisholm, Renty Fields, William Ferguson, Jeffrey Buncombe, William Smiley, David Heyward, Christopher Bryan, Theodore Wilson and William Lightburn.

The deed for the property was recorded in the courthouse of Beaufort County on December 4, 1847. The cornerstone was laid in 1891 under Reverend Hollam. The church was renamed Campbell Chapel in honor of J.P. Campbell, the 8th Bishop of the A.M.E. Church, who was presiding over South Carolina at the time.

The original building has been altered as follows:

- The building was extended to the rear, a choir loft was added, the church was re-floored and a brick step built under the leadership of Reverend James Bumcombe.
- An annex was added in 1966 containing classrooms and a kitchen.
- The sanctuary was completely renovated in 1973 under the leadership of Reverend L.T. Baker.

# Appendix C

African Methodist Episcopal Religion

&

Richard Allen

Notes taken from http://www.mtherbethel.org/museum.htm

Mother Bethel
African Methodist Episcopal Church

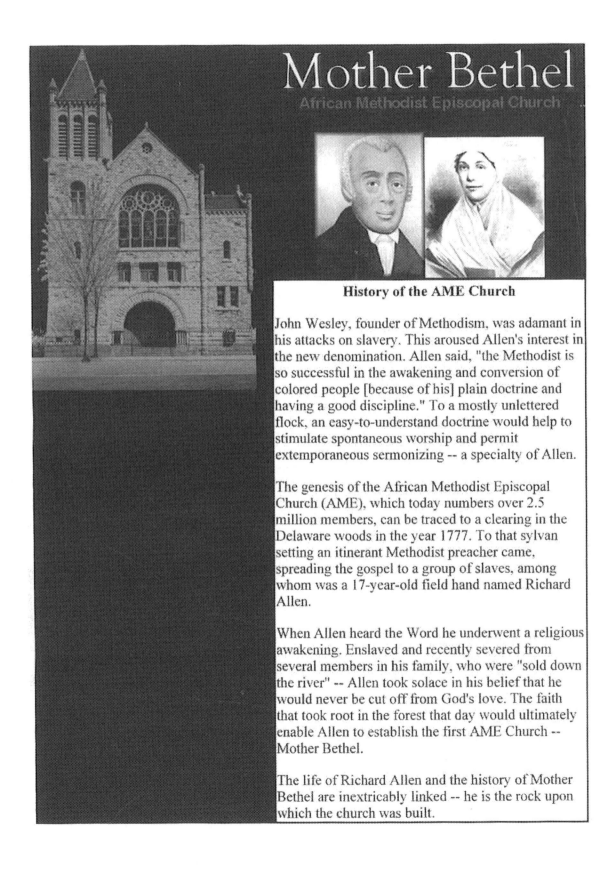

# Mother Bethel
## African Methodist Episcopal Church

**History of the AME Church**

John Wesley, founder of Methodism, was adamant in his attacks on slavery. This aroused Allen's interest in the new denomination. Allen said, "the Methodist is so successful in the awakening and conversion of colored people [because of his] plain doctrine and having a good discipline." To a mostly unlettered flock, an easy-to-understand doctrine would help to stimulate spontaneous worship and permit extemporaneous sermonizing -- a specialty of Allen.

The genesis of the African Methodist Episcopal Church (AME), which today numbers over 2.5 million members, can be traced to a clearing in the Delaware woods in the year 1777. To that sylvan setting an itinerant Methodist preacher came, spreading the gospel to a group of slaves, among whom was a 17-year-old field hand named Richard Allen.

When Allen heard the Word he underwent a religious awakening. Enslaved and recently severed from several members in his family, who were "sold down the river" -- Allen took solace in his belief that he would never be cut off from God's love. The faith that took root in the forest that day would ultimately enable Allen to establish the first AME Church -- Mother Bethel.

The life of Richard Allen and the history of Mother Bethel are inextricably linked -- he is the rock upon which the church was built.

Richard Allen was born into the slave-owning, Philadelphia household of Benjamin Chew in 1760. Chew was a successful lawyer who would become Pennsylvania's attorney general and chief justice of the court of appeals. (Chew's country estate, Cliveden, became the focal point of the 1777 Battle of Germantown.) Allen and his parents and siblings were household slaves of the Chews, responsible for cleaning, cooking and looking after the family's five children.

When Richard was 7, he and his entire family were sold to a Delaware farmer named Stokeley Sturgis. While he was lucky in that his family was kept intact, he now had to endure the arduous life of a field hand. In recalling his masters at a later period in life, he called them "kind" but said slavery was a "bitter pill." The pill became more bitter after Sturgis sold Richard's mother and three siblings. Allen, 17 at the time, would never see these family members again.

After his forest revelation in Delaware, Allen would regularly (and furtively) meet in the woods with preacher John Gray and others. Delaware law forbade blacks from congregating without whites present. Circuit preachers such as Gray offered hope, eternal salvation, and abolitionism's promise to blacks. Most appealing to Allen personally were the call for discipline and individual responsibility, and the fiery nature of the preachers.

**FREEDOM**

Master Sturgis came to feel that slaves were better workers because of Christianity -- a lesson taught him by Richard Allen. As such, when Allen requested that Reverend Freeborn Garrettson be allowed to preach at the farm, Sturgis acceded. Garrettson was a former slave owner who now preached abolition. His sermon at the farm that day was based on Daniel 5:27, the verse in which God's handwriting appears on the wall to Babylonian King Belshazzar.

Part of the writing on the wall translates to: "Thou art weighed in the balances, and art found wanting." The preacher with the remarkably apt Christian name believed the sin of slaveholding was so onerous that on Judgment Day all slave owners would be weighed and be found wanting.

A shaken Sturgis decided that he would free Allen. But, he was debt-ridden and couldn't afford to do so. He agreed to allow Allen to buy his own freedom for $2,000. Allen worked nights and at off-hours cutting cord wood and doing odd jobs. By the time he was 20, he bought his freedom.

Work, however, was scarce for free blacks. Initially, Allen found employment in a brickyard. During the Revolutionary War, Allen was a teamster, hauling salt from Reheboth, Delaware, to Valley Forge. At this time Allen also started preaching. After the war Allen taught the gospel extensively in Delaware, Maryland, and Pennsylvania, preaching to mixed gatherings of blacks and whites. A Radnor, Pennsylvania, salvation seeker commented, "This man must be a man of God, I never heard such preaching before."

Allen started following the Methodist circuit and is believed to have been in attendance at the Christmas conference of 1784 when Methodism established itself as a denomination distinct from the Church of England. Bishop Francis Asbury, the moving force behind American Methodism (he traveled over 100,000 miles to spread the gospel), asked Richard Allen to accompany him on a preaching trip through the South. Allen declined. Not only would the trip be dangerous for a black man, Allen knew that sleeping in a coach and other indignities that he would be subject to would set a poor example of behavior by a freed black man to those still enslaved.

## BACK TO PHILLY

Philadelphia's St. George's, America's first Methodist church (and today the world's oldest Methodist church in continuous service), invited Allen to preach. Thus, in 1786, Allen returned to the city of his birth. In Philadelphia, Allen found a city where almost 70 percent of the blacks were free. He started preaching regularly at Sunday 5 A.M. services, though he found this an uncomfortable time to be at the pulpit. Allen would then preach three or four more sermons at different churches every Sunday. Allen's preaching was so successful that new members joined St. George's weekly, building particularly the black portion of the congregation.

In Allen's own words, he appealed to his "African brethren, who had been a long forgotten people," few of whom attended public worship. White leaders at St. George's viewed the new influx of black parishioners warily. Black members of the congregation were forced to sit toward the back of the church during prayers and were sometimes made to stand. Recognizing that black congregants had special spiritual needs, and that the white congregants were growing uneasy with the burgeoning black population in the church, Allen approached the elder at St. George's and asked his permission in establishing a black church. The elder denied his request. In a year's time a new elder again denied Allen's request, and also rebuffed Allen stridently with what Allen called "very degrading and insulting language."

**FREE AFRICAN SOCIETY**

To counteract the baleful influence of St. George's, Allen, along with Absalom Jones, came together to form the Free African Society (FAS) on April 12, 1787. The Society, though not religiously affiliated, proved much like a church in serving the black community. NAACP founder, W.E.B. DuBois, writing a century later, called the FAS, "the first wavering step of a people toward organized social life." Organized as an altruistic society for extending mutual aid to the widowed, sick, and jobless, it was funded by dues-paying members. The core of Allen's beliefs can be summarized with his trust that members by lifting themselves would lift all black people. The society also regulated marriages, taught thrift, censured drunkenness, condemned adultery, and attempted to improve morals.

**THE SPLIT FROM ST. GEORGE'S**

Back at St. George's, interracial tensions increased. Growing membership necessitated a church expansion. Black church members were the most generous contributors of time and money to help build a new gallery. What they did not know was that the expanded upper gallery was targeted exclusively for the growing black membership. On a November Sunday in 1787, at the first Sabbath service after the church's renovations, a sexton ushered Allen, Absalom Jones, and prominent black church member William White to seats in the new gallery which was situated above the old part of the church. As the trio was a little late, they instead took seats near where they had formerly sat before the renovation. The service started and the congregation dropped to their knees in prayer.

An altercation ensued.

Allen looked up to find a church trustee trying to wrench Absalom Jones to his feet. It seemed that blacks were not to sit in the old gallery but to be relegated to the new gallery. An astonished Jones said to the trustee, "Wait until the prayer is over." The martinet replied, "No, you must get now, or I will call for aid and force you away." The devout Jones replied, "Wait until the prayer is over, and I will get up and trouble you no more." Then another trustee came and tried to pull William White from his knees. Allen recalled, "By this time the prayer was over, and we all went out of the church in a body, and they were no more plagued by us in the church."

**BACK TO THE FREE AFRICAN SOCIETY**

Those blacks who left St. George's turned to the Free African Society as a de facto church. Allen helped to minister to the spiritual needs of those in the group. Over time, the FAS began to take on trappings of Quaker culture. Quakers were admired for their abolitionist views, philanthropy, and moral rectitude. In fact, the FAS charter mandated that all treasurers of the society were to be Quakers. This would facilitate the Society's dealings with financial institutions.

Allen, however, was disenchanted with the Society's mirroring of Quaker ways, finding them inimical with what he felt blacks needed spiritually.

Beginning each meeting with a Quaker-like silence of 15 minutes, for instance, was diametrically opposed to the spontaneity and exuberant atmosphere of Methodist services. Unable to embrace the ways of the FAS, Allen was "read out" of the society on June 20, 1789.

Leadership of the Society fell to fellow Methodist Absalom Jones who felt it was important that those in the Society be spiritually attended to. Jones began to draw up a subscription list for the building of a church for the society's members. Though Allen was disassociated from the FAS he enthusiastically supported the plan to form the nation's first black church. Several whites, including Robert Ralston, Benjamin "the father of American Medicine" Rush, and a different William White, the Bishop of the Episcopal church, threw both financial and moral support behind the project.

Allen was given the responsibility of buying land for the church. Laying out his own money, Allen purchased a plot of land at 6th and Lombard in Philadelphia's already historic black community. As a note, during his early years in Philadelphia, Allen supported himself as a chimney sweep and parlayed his earnings into a shoemaking shop which eventually employed several apprentices. He was practicing the diligence and ethos of hard work that he preached. The disciplined preacher ultimately became a rather prosperous Philadelphian, donating almost $10,000 to the AME church.

Allen now owned this property, but the FAS decided that they wanted their church built outside the black community, on Fifth Street, south of Walnut Street, in a mostly white neighborhood. Groundbreaking was in 1791 and Allen enjoyed the honor of breaking earth on the project.

Yet, it was still unclear what denomination the church would be. Since the black walkout at St. George's, the white Methodists had increased the hostility aimed at the splinter group while still trying to lure them back in the fold. Elders at St. George's saw their authority threatened, and in turn threatened to expel the exiles permanently. Allen replied that they could not be part of a church where they had been so "scandalously treated." He addressed St. George's Reverend McCloskey, saying, "If you deny us your name [Methodism] you cannot seal up the scripture from us, and deny us a name in heaven." The FAS voted to be Episcopalian even though Jones and Allen wanted it to be Methodist. Absalom Jones agreed to head what would be called the Saint

Thomas African Episcopal Church. In 1804, Jones would go on to be ordained the first black priest in the United States. W.E.B. DuBois said of Saint Thomas's: "the church has always been foremost in good work." Officers from St. Thomas's went on to found the nation's first black insurance firm.

Allen, however, was still convinced that the discipline and style of Methodism was best suited to the black community in Philadelphia. "The plain and simple gospel suits best for the people -- for the unlearned can understand and the learned are sure to understand." Allen was willing to wait until St. Thomas's was completed before building his church. Why would the FAS opt for the Episcopal church? The hostility of the Methodists contrasted with the largess of Bishop White and the Episcopals. Further, there was antipathy in some members of the FAS toward dance and song traditionally associated with the Methodists. One member is quoted as saying, "It was a shameful practice that we, as a people are guilty of. While we are feasting and dancing many of our complexion are starving under cruel bondage; because of this practice of ours that enables our enemies to declare that we are not fit for freedom."

**YELLOW FEVER**

Before St. Thomas's was completed, the Yellow Fever epidemic of 1793 intervened. The great plague decimated Philadelphia, killing 5,000 of its 50,000 inhabitants. Dr. Benjamin Rush and Mayor Matthew Clarkson asked Allen and Jones for their help in fighting the dread disease. It was thought that blacks were less likely to get the fever, though it was believed they were not wholly immune from it. Of course, this is not true.

The pair overcame their dread fear and "found freedom to go forth, confiding in Him who can preserve in the midst of a burning, fiery furnace." They found in the first house they visited two children huddled with their feverish father, their mother already a victim. Jones and Allen found people to care for the children and tried to aid the sick father. A score more visits awaited the preachers in that first day alone. In the following weeks Allen organized dead-removal crews and continued to assist doctors. Allen was even taught by Benjamin

Rush how to "bleed" fever victims, the treatment thought most efficacious by the eminent physician. Despite their best efforts, Jones and Allen were the subject of a bilious attack by Mathew Carey (whose name is associated with America's oldest publishing house) who accused blacks of profiting financially from Yellow Fever. According to Carey, Allen's crew of blacks overcharged for body removal and stole goods from the houses they entered. Mayor Clarkson and Richard Allen took out ads in newspapers denouncing Carey and his accusations.

**BETHEL CHURCH**
Ironically the Yellow Fever epidemic allowed black and white Philadelphians to see Allen's altruistic soul in action. Tensions between Allen and St. George's cooled -- and he received permission from them to build a church on the site where he purchased the land for St. Thomas's years earlier. While funds were being raised to build a permanent structure, Allen bought a blacksmith shop from a fellow named Sims and had it hauled by a team of his own horses to 6th and Lombard. Bishop Asbury presided over the church's dedication on July 29, 1794. Reverend Dickins of St. George's suggested the name Bethel, meaning "the house of the Lord." Years later, W.E.B. DuBois called Mother Bethel, "by long odds the vastest and most remarkable product of American Negro civilization."

**ALLEN AND HIS CRITICS**
Allen still had his critics. William Douglass, a pastor at St. Thomas's, said Methodism "appealed chiefly to the feelings and affectations which are always strongest among undisciplined minds." Moreover, the blacks who remained at St. George's after the 1787 schism accused Allen of segregating the race. Then there was the constant struggle with trustees at St. George's who attempted to control Mother Bethel's affairs. In 1796, for instance, St. George's wanted Bethel's property to pass to the Methodist conference. A trustee from St. George's by the name of Ezekiel Cooper tricked Richard Allen into signing over Bethel's land during incorporation. In 1807, members of Bethel drew up what Allen called the African

Supplement, which attempted to throw off the yoke of St. George's. The Supplement gave trustees, "the right to nominate and appoint one or more persons of the African race to exhort and preach in Bethel Church and any other church which may hereafter become the property of the corporation..."

Despite these conflicts, Bethel grew. In its first two years, membership mushroomed from 20 to 121. Thanks to Allen's insistence on education Bethel had a children's day school and an adult night school on premises soon after its founding. In 1799, Richard Allen was ordained a deacon.

## SLAVE SPECULATOR

One day in 1808, a slave speculator came to the Bethel church door with a constable saying that Allen was a runaway slave. Slave speculators were a breed of men who bought the rights to escaped slaves, captured them, and resold them in the South. Other speculators would simply kidnap free blacks and sell them into slavery. This was a particularly simple-minded slave speculator, as most of Philadelphia would vouch that Richard Allen lived in the city for nearly 20 years and had not escaped from the South just a few years earlier as the speculator claimed. Allen sued the speculator for false accusation and perjury. The man could not make the $800 bail and was thrown into the Walnut Street Prison. From then on Allen redoubled his efforts in helping runaway slaves.

## THE UNDERGROUND RAILROAD

Richard Allen preached abolition. One weapon he used in fighting slavery was pamphlets. In a pamphlet addressed to slave-owners, Allen claimed bondage was anti-American and anti-Bible. In another pamphlet addressed to blacks he exhorted all freed black men to help their enslaved brethren by being exemplary citizens and offering direct assistance.

As early as 1795, Allen helped 30 recently freed Jamaican slaves who had newly arrived in Philadelphia. It fell upon Allen to take care of them by finding housing and providing food.

As some point, the church's basement was used as a stop on the Underground Railroad (a network of houses creating a link from the south to Canada, where escaped slaves would be allowed to remain free). Aided in great part by his wife Sarah, Allen would hide, feed and clothe escaping slaves. Large sums of money were collected in order to facilitate a slave's flight to freedom. Some current members of the Mother Bethel AME church are descendants of those who were escaped slaves assisted by Mother Bethel.

## MORE CONFRONTATIONS

In 1815, the elders at St. George's managed to get Bethel put up for auction. Allen was forced to buy back his own church for the obscenely high price of $10,125. Shortly thereafter, a preacher from St. George's went to court claiming he had a right to preach at Bethel. The court disagreed saying, "what right do you have to preach to a congregation that won't listen to you." This was the de facto independence ruling for Bethel.

## A CHURCH IS BORN

The next year the Bethelites won a court case recognizing their right to exist as an independent denomination. On April 9, 1816, at Bethel Church, Allen called together Black Methodist Episcopal churches to a conference in Philadelphia. Allen decided the time had come for these churches to band together. "Resolved, that the people of Philadelphia, Baltimore and other places who may unite with them shall become one body under the name and style of the African Methodist Church of the United States of American and that the book of Discipline of the Methodist Episcopal Church be adopted as our discipline..." Thus, Bethel Church became Mother Bethel African Methodist Episcopal Church. Allen commented, "We deemed it expedient to have a form of discipline, whereby we may guide our people in the fear of God, in the unity of the Spirit, and in the bonds of peace." They adopted the episcopal form of church government -- meaning they would be under the authority of bishops who were ordained by officials within. At that meeting Allen was elected the first Bishop of the AME church.

## BACK TO AFRICA

Bishop Allen confronted a new threat soon after. The American Colonization Society was an all-white group which included Henry Clay, Andrew Jackson, James Madison, and Thomas Jefferson, who endorsed black emigration to Africa either through voluntary means or through forceful deportation. Clay called blacks "pernicious and useless, if not dangerous." Jefferson said, "Let the ocean divide the white man from the man of color."

Allen called a mass meeting of the black Philadelphia community to oppose this. Allen feared that if the black community supported this movement there would be no one left to aid slaves and also felt blacks should be treated as American citizens with all attendant rights. He wrote, "Whereas our ancestors (not of choice) were the first successful cultivators of the wilds of America, we their descendants feel ourselves entitled to participate in the blessings of her soil, which their blood and sweat manured." Due to the efforts of Allen and other black leaders, the Colonization movement lost momentum after a number of years.

Allen remained influential to the end of his life. In 1830, Mother Bethel hosted the first national convention of black Americans, which led to the formation of the American Society of Free Persons of Colour. The meeting was called to establish a national network of black support and to fight new and heinous actions by the American Colonization Society, and to fight slavery.

One of Allen's last major accomplishments was the formation of the Free Produce Society in December 1830. Members of the society pledged to buy only products made by non-slave labor, whenever possible. Initially advocated by the abolitionist William Lloyd Garrison, the boycott also served as an exhibition of black self-reliance. One of Allen's last lessons was the economic power of boycotting, a favorite weapon of the Civil Rights Movement of the 1960s.

Allen died on March 26, 1831, after "a tedious illness," as his tomb notes. He had the largest black funeral that America had ever seen. Encomia poured forth. William Lloyd Garrison called Allen "one of the purest friends and patriots that ever exerted his energies in favor of civil and religious liberty. His noble deeds will remain cherished in the memory of mankind as imperishable monuments of eternal glory."

Perhaps it was David Walker, a radical abolitionist, who had best understood Allen's significance. Walker, in his 1829 "Appeal to the Coloured Citizens of the Worlds," a vitriolic attack on slavery, wrote of Allen: "When the Lord shall raise up colured historians in succeeding generations, to present the crimes of this nation, to the then gazing world, the Holy Ghost will make them do justice to the name of Bishop Allen. He will stand on the pages of history among the greatest divines who have lived since the apostolic age."

## THE CHURCH TODAY

Of special interest are the church's stained glass windows. Installed when the church was erected in 1890, they were produced by the Century Art Company at a cost of $1,190. They are brimming with symbolism. In the words of church historian Ruby Boyd, the windows are "sermons in art." The five windows on the church's Pine Street side depict Biblical references. The windows on the Richard Allen Avenue side are devoted to Jesus Christ. On the Lombard Street side, one of the windows makes significant use of Masonic symbols and was indeed donated by a Masonic order. The second Prince Hall Masonic Lodge in the United States was founded at Mother Bethel. Prince Hall was a noted black Boston abolitionist. //

## THE RICHARD ALLEN MUSEUM

On the lower level of Mother Bethel is an inspirational three-room museum.

The first room of the museum contains sketches and photographs of all the AME bishops. Also in the first room are platters and pieces from a tea set that belonged to Allen.

It is in the museum's middle room that the power and grace of Richard Allen is most keenly felt. There one finds an unpolished wooden pulpit which was used in the original blacksmith's-shop-turned-church and several pews used in that structure as well. The unadorned pews seem more like benches in a one-room schoolhouse; the pulpit rises above the pews like a teacher's rostrum. The effect is one of intimacy, immediacy, and family.

Allen used his carpentry skills to fashion the pulpit (which was once the centerpiece of a Smithsonian exhibition) himself. Next to the pulpit are Allen's own pulpit chair (originally held together with wooden pegs) and his prayer stools. On the opposite side of the room are the pews which were in the second church as well. Along one wall is a "moaner's bench," used by those in the congregation who sat on it until they felt the spirit enter them. Penitents praying for salvation also used the moaner's bench. Displayed on a wall is Richard Allen's own Bible which is believed to have been printed in the 1600s. This Bible is so worn from use and time that the age and beauty of its binding is equaled by its conspicuous use. Above the Bible are tickets from an 1818 "love feast" -- a prayer and praise service -- which was held at Mother Bethel every Tuesday night. Only those who went to the Tuesday love feast and received tickets were allowed to receive communion on the following Sunday. Above the tickets is a "License to Exhorte." Signed by Richard Allen in 1819, it permitted Noah Cannon the right to preach in the African Methodist Church for one year. Also in the middle room is a "Proclamation to all the Good People of Massachusetts!" dated April 4, 1851. In effect, the proclamation was a wanted poster used to warn Bay State residents that slave hunters were among them, attempting to steal free blacks and sell them into slavery. Vividly described are three slave hunters, among them one John Bacon, who had a "red, intemperate looking face and a retreating forehead. His hair is dark and a little gray. He wears a black coat, mixed pants, and a purplish vest. He looks sleepy and yet malicious at the same time." Another, a man just called Davis, was "an unusually ill-looking fellow...He has a Roman nose, one of his eyes has been knocked out. He looks like a Pirate, and knows how to be a Stealer of Men."

On another wall of the second room are three muskets believed to have been used by a militia raised by Richard Allen and Absalom Jones for the defense of Philadelphia during the War of 1812. Asked by the mayor to form a black regiment, the preaching pair mustered 2,500 troops whose barracks were in Southwest Philadelphia. They saw no action in the war, however.

Of great interest in the museum's third room is a ballot box in which marbles were used to cast votes. In the church's early years many members were unable to read or write. To elect church trustees, a box with pictures of the candidates was used. Underneath each picture was a hole drilled into the box. Marbles were dropped into these holes under the picture of the office-seeker being voted for.

Drawings and pictures of the four Bethel churches located at this site are seen on the wall. The first, as you recall, was the blacksmith shop hauled to this site by horses. The second church, the first built on the site, was called Roughcast because it was built from crude cinder blocks. The Roughcast church saw the organization of the AME denomination. It was used between 1805 and 1841. The third church, built in 1841, bears more than a passing similarity to St. George's. The fourth and present church was dedicated on October 2, 1889; the chief architect was Edward Hazlehurst.

Also in the third room of the museum is a poster bearing suggested rules of behavior. One of the rules urged gentleman not to spit on the floor but to use spittoons instead. Another rule asked gentleman to leave church by the north door and not to crowd the ladies' passageway.

Great leaders in AME's history are also celebrated in the third room. A lithograph of Morris Brown, the fourth pastor of Mother Bethel, tells of his remarkable exploits. Brown developed a significant congregation of free blacks in the early 1800s and ushered them into the AME flock. He took part in the failed Denmark Vesey uprising of 1822 and escaped to Philadelphia. He ultimately became the second Bishop of the AME church.

Also honored is Fannie Coppin (1835-1912) who was the first president of the Institute for Colored Youth, a Normal School supported by the Quakers. Cheyney State College is today an outgrowth of that organization. In addition to recommending that blacks be trained in trades and industrial arts, she also considered the classics an integral part of a curriculum.

**ALLENS' TOMB**

Richard and Sarah Allen are interred on the church's lower level. A lengthy inscription on the tomb includes the following: "He was instrumental in the hands of the lord in enlightening many thousands of his brethren, the descendants of Africa, and was the founder of the first African Church in America."

------------------------------------------------

Mother Bethel Church was a stop on the Underground Railroad.

AME is the second-oldest black congregation (after St. Thomas's in Philadelphia) in the country.

The ground on which Mother Bethel stands is the oldest parcel of real estate continuously owned by African-Americans in the United States.

The second Prince Hall Masonic Lodge was founded here.

Lucretia Mott, abolitionist and women's rights advocate, abolitionist and journalist Frederick Douglass, and William Still, a moving force behind the Underground Railroad, were among those who spoke from the rostrum at Mother Bethel.

Ben Franklin contributed money to the African Methodist Episcopal Church.

A female Mother Bethel preacher, Jarena Lee, was one of first black women to speak out publicly against slavery.

Richard Allen was a frequent contributor to the "Freedom's Journal," the first newspaper in American to be owned and published by blacks.

On the lower level, a James Dupree mural depicts the history of the church.

The first black boy scout troop was founded at Mother Bethel Church.·

Today the AME Church comprises 2.5 million members, 8,000 ministers, and 6,200 congregations in 19 Episcopal districts and hosts 115 annual conferences.

------------------------------------------------

Location: 419 Richard Allen Avenue at the northeast corner of Sixth and Richard Allen Avenue (Lombard Street between Fifth and Sixth Streets).

First Church on site: 1794

Present Church Built: 1889-90

# Appendix D

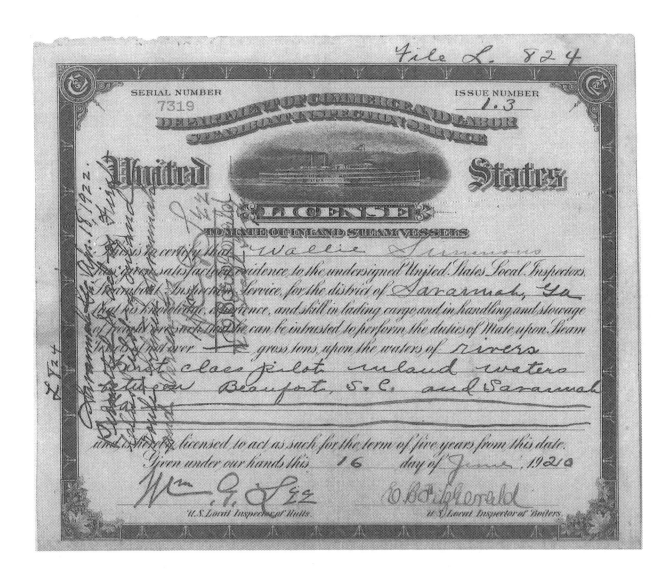

Printed in the United States
By Bookmasters